MAKING
Miniature
Villages
IN
Polymer Clay

Gail Ritchey

NORTH LIGHT BOOKS
CINCINNATI, OHIO

www.nlbooks.com

ABOUT THE AUTHOR

Gail Ritchey started her designing career by creating a series of licensed cross-stitch designs of Lilliput Lane Cottages for her company, Cottage Fever.

Gail was introduced to polymer clay at a Society of Craft Designers' seminar. She spent several years playing with this medium until she found her "niche" in 1997: Gail's miniature clay cottages combine her loves of architecture and collectibles.

In 1998, one of Gail's cottages won the grand prize in the professional division of FIMO's "Jetting to Germany" contest.

Gail is a member of the Society of Craft Designers and the Polymer Clay Guild.

She is married and has one daughter, three sons and two grandsons. She loves to promote crafting for all, but especially for children.

Other fine North Light Books are available from your local bookstore, art supply store or direct from the publisher.

04 03 02 01 00   5 4 3 2 1

Library of Congress Cataloging-in-Publication Data

Ritchey, Gail
    Making miniature villages in polymer clay / Gail Ritchey.—1st ed.
        p.   cm.
    Includes index.
    ISBN 0-89134-956-1 (pbk.: alk. paper)
    1. Polymer clay craft. 2. Miniature craft. 3. Cities and towns in art. I. Title.
TT297.R58 2000
745.5928—dc21
                            99-36221
                             CIP

Editor: Jennifer Long
Cover designer: Stephanie Strang
Interior designer: Brian Roeth
Interior production: Ruth Preston
Production Coordinator: Emily Gross
Cover photography: Greg Grosse
Chapter opener photography: Christine Polomsky
Finished village photography, pages 126–127: Al Parrish

DEDICATION

I want to dedicate this book to my family: To my parents, who gave me the courage to try to do anything I wanted. My mother was always proud of me and my efforts and gave me a lot of encouragement. My father taught me to think by giving me jobs to do, but not telling me how to do them. Dad would then walk by and say, "There is an easier way to do that," and walk away. Later, he would come back and say things like, "Yes, that's it," or "Try harder," or even, "That is an even better way to do it than I thought of." Because of that training, I knew that if I gave it enough thought, I would come up with a way to create my cottage designs in polymer clay that would be easy enough for any crafter to follow.

I also want to dedicate this book to my husband, Terry, who has encouraged and backed me throughout my career. And to my children, who have also encouraged Mom and have shown that they are proud of her. (Especially Adam, who is my biggest critic. When he says, "That's great, Mom!" I know that I can stop working on that problem and go on to the next.)

ACKNOWLEDGMENTS

I want to thank Greg Albert, Editorial Director of North Light Books, for taking a chance on my book and on a new author, and Jennifer Long for giving me the encouragement to finish it.

I want to thank my husband, Terry, for supporting me and doing my photography, and my children for putting up with a Mom who was there, but not there.

I also want to thank one of my designing friends, Linda Wyszynski, for giving me the courage to try this. Her support throughout this book has been invaluable. When I felt like giving up, she was always there to give me a little extra push.

Finally, I want to thank polymer clay artists and authors Maureen Carlson and Donna Kato for giving of themselves and for their hints, tips and inspiration. You are wonderful.

Thanks, all.

table of contents

For as long as I can remember, I have loved to create things. I started by making "tied on" clothes for my dolls, even before my mother would let me use a needle. Later, my grandmother taught me crochet and many other crafts, my father's Aunt Mary taught me how to knit and I joined 4-H to learn how to sew. Next, I learned how to cross-stitch and eventually started designing cross-stitch cottages for my own company, Cottage Fever.

Then I was introduced to polymer clay. I loved it! Polymer clay is such fun to work with; I got satisfaction from kneading it, feeling it and creating with it. I was hooked. I played with polymer clay for several years in between my other craft-designing efforts. Since I love miniature houses and villages, I thought and thought (thanks, Dad) about how I could create my own miniature village in polymer clay.

My first efforts were all right, but it would have been very difficult for me to give instructions to others so that they could recreate the cottages. I spent about two years trying different techniques for creating my village before I came up with an easy way. This book is the result of all my efforts.

The cottages in this book may look difficult, but they are actually very easy to do. You will bake them in stages so that the foundation you are working on is already hardened and you are just adding another layer. My twelve-year-old made a cottage of his own design that looks great.

A note of encouragement: I am an idea person, not a perfectionist. I love the challenge of trying to figure out a way to do something or how to achieve a certain look. Once I figure out how to handle a challenge, my mind jumps to the next problem, and I have to force myself to finish the first task. Therefore, the majority of you will make cottages that will look even better than mine!

Try creating your own village. The first cottage may be a challenge, but as you get the hang of it, it will get easier and easier. The important thing is to start. Remember to have fun, and when you're done, you'll have something to be proud of.

chapter one

What is Polymer Clay?

Polymer clay is a wonderful, man-made material that hardens in your home oven. There are three major manufacturers of colored polymer clays. Eberhard Faber, a German company, makes FIMO and FIMO Soft. Cernit is also made in Germany. Sculpey III and Premo are manufactured in the United States by the Polyform Company. These companies also produce clays that can be used for doll making and other crafts.

All three clays are similar in that they need to be conditioned, or softened, by kneading with your hands, you can mix any of the colors and you bake them in your oven to harden. The differences in the three polymer clays are in their firmness in their original state and how hard they become when baked.

FIMO is the firmest clay and takes longest to condition, but holds its shape best when worked with. It is fairly hard when baked and comes in fifty-six colors. Because I use very thin sheets of clay on my cottages, I prefer FIMO. See the tips in chapter two for ways to ease the conditioning of this clay.

FIMO Soft is softer than regular FIMO, but is still slightly firmer than the other polymer clays I use. FIMO Soft comes in twelve colors.

Cernit is softer and easier to condition than either of the FIMO clays, but gets sticky if worked with too long. It is the hardest clay when baked. Cernit comes in forty-four colors, including wonderful metallics.

Sculpey III is very soft and takes almost no conditioning; however, if you're mixing colors, by the time they are mixed, the clay will be very soft and will fingerprint easily. Sculpey III is not as hard when baked as the previous brands. It comes in forty colors.

Premo is another clay by the Polyform Company. It's similar to Sculpey III in texture, but remains flexible when baked. It comes in thirty-two colors.

Any of the polymer clays should work with my cottages. Use the clay you prefer, modifying my techniques to suit the characteristics of your favorite clay. Test the baking temperature and time for the clay you are using—some of the clays may scorch if baked too long.

Whichever clay you choose, have fun making your own cottages.

chapter two

Tools, Tips & Techniques

TOOLS

You will not need many tools to make the projects in this book. Following are descriptions of the few tools that are absolutely necessary, as well as some others that are helpful.

CUTTING TOOLS

All of the following cutting tools are very sharp; care must be taken when using them. One of the most necessary cutting tools is a craft knife. I use it continually. Although you could use a sharp kitchen knife, the blade will dull as you use it. The blade on a craft knife can be easily changed when it becomes dull.

Another cutting tool that I use frequently is a homemade chisel. Chisel blades are inexpensive and come in two sizes: ³⁄₁₆" (.5 cm) and ¼" (.6 cm).

I made my own handle from clay, inserted a chisel blade and baked it for thirty minutes. Be sure to check the package of the clay you are using for the recommended temperature. If you don't have a chisel blade, use your craft knife when the project instructions call for a chisel.

The third type of cutting tool that I use is a slicing blade. Slicing blades are great for cutting the base walls and roof pieces, giving you a nice, straight cut without pulling the clay.

There are several slicing blades on the market, but the one I prefer is the NuBlade. This 6" (15.2 cm) blade lasts longer than other blades. This blade is very sharp, so please be very careful when using it! Put a clay handle along the dull side of the blade and bake it for thirty minutes. This immediately lets you know which side is the sharp one. (If you use the blade for cutting mille-fiori or other items that are thicker than what I'm cutting in this book, you can put clay handles on just the corners.)

To cover the sharp edge of the blade when not in use, I cut a piece of the plastic strip from a report cover holder.

A slicing blade really makes creating the cottages easier; I would recommend you try to get one.

NEEDLE TOOLS

You can purchase needle tools or make your own. Several different sizes and points are used in this book, from sharps to dull darning needles. To make them easier to use, make a polymer clay handle for each. Insert the needle in the handle and bake it for thirty minutes at the recommended temperature.

STYLUS

Another useful tool is a stylus. This is like a needle tool with a ball on one or both ends. They come in many sizes and can be found at most craft and art supply stores.

CLAY SHAPER TOOL

Clay Shapers are rubber-tipped tools that can be used to shape and press your clay pieces together without leaving fingerprints. I use my Clay Shaper to press leaves and flowers onto the cottages. They're also helpful in getting the clay smooth or into small or hard-to-reach places, like under a roof.

Shown here, clockwise from the top, are my slicing blades, a craft knife, my needle tools and my chisel tools.

SCRATCH TOOLS

The scratch tools are useful for creating textures on your polymer clay. When I first started making these cottages, I made my own scratch tools by cutting pieces of wire and baking them into a clay handle. You can also use a wire brush, but they are harder to get into crevices.

BRUSHES

A soft brush, such as a blush makeup brush, is handy for brushing crumbs off the clay and for dusting your master-pieces.

PATTERN CUTTERS AND EXTRUDERS

A handy set of tools to own are Kemper Pattern Cutters. For the projects in this book, I use a 3/16" (.5 cm) set of cutters that includes a circle, a teardrop, a heart and a flower cutter.

To create very small "snakes" (rolls or strings of clay), you can use a garlic press or Klay Gun. The Klay Gun comes with nineteen different discs to make different shapes.

A rotary cutter is good for straight cuts; the pattern blades can be used to make uniquely-shaped edges.

ROLLING TOOLS

The one tool I can't do without is my pasta machine. It's great for creating smooth sheets of polymer clay.

You can also use a brayer or rolling pin for making sheets of polymer clay. I've found I can't get even sheets of clay with a brayer, but then I can't make pie crusts, either!

If you are going to make several cottages, do your best to find a pasta machine. Check garage sales, ask friends if they have one they don't use, ask for one for a gift, or just go purchase one for yourself.

Your pasta machine will pay for itself by saving you time and lots of work rolling clay.

Clockwise from the top are a soft paint brush, two types of stylus, some of my texture tools (wire brushes, toothpicks and precision screw-drivers), my Clay Shaper tool, and a blush brush.

Clockwise from the right are my Fiskars Rotary Cutter with different blades, a pastry cutter, my Kemper Pattern Cutters, my Klay Gun with an assort-ment of extruders and a garlic press.

This is my favorite tool of all — my pasta machine — and a brayer.

MEASURING TOOLS

To measure your polymer clay, use a circle template. They can be purchased at office supply stores.

There is also a new measuring tool on the market, designed by Diana Crick for American Art Clay Co., Inc. (AMACO), that has circles for measuring balls of clay. You can also use it to measure some sizes by setting a whole block of polymer clay on the template.

If you have one of these templates, I have given you additional combinations to get some of the ball sizes not given on the template. (See page 124.)

You can also use a ruler to measure polymer clay. Check page 11 for instructions.

Another tool that is sometimes used to measure clay is a Marxit. This plastic tool has marks on the side that give different measurements.

THE CLAY WARMER

Warming clay helps to soften or condition it, making it easier to extrude or mix with other colors.

Place the Clay Warmer in your microwave to heat it. After it is warmed, remove it from the microwave and place your clay inside.

I use this anytime I am using the Klay Gun to warm the gun with the clay inside. If you can't find a Clay Warmer, just cover a medical hot/cold pack with a towel and warm it in the microwave. Do not microwave the polymer clay.

FOOD PROCESSOR

You can make conditioning polymer clay and mixing colors easier by running the clay through a food processor dedicated to clay work. The processor will chop the clay into small pieces and start to warm it. After processing, put the clay into a plastic bag and knead until the pieces stick together. Do not use the food processor for food after processing polymer clay in it.

PLASTIC BAGS

A plastic bag is a great way to store your polymer clay. It keeps the clay clean, and you can sort it by color and type.

I prefer to use the GladLock Zipper Storage Bags; they have a strip at the top that you can write on.

Polymer clay will dissolve rigid plastic. Do not store your clay in a hard plastic container.

TEXTURE TOOLS

My favorite tool for texturing clay is a Scotch-Brite pad. Another item I use is a

The tools, shown from left to right, are the snack bags I prefer, my food processor (used for clay only), a Marxit, my Clay Warmer, a couple of circle templates and a ruler.

Here is the parchment paper, an oven thermometer, the Scotch-Brite pads, ceramic tiles and a rubber mat.

nylon vegetable bag.

Different fabrics are also great for texturing clay. Look around your home for other items with interesting textures.

RUBBER MAT

A piece of rubber mat or rubber shelf liner is great for keeping your ceramic tile and Klay Gun from sliding around on your work surface.

BAKING TOOLS

A ceramic tile is a great baking surface for polymer clay. You can do your clay work on it and then bake the piece on the same tile without having to move the item. I have a collection of 4" (10.2 cm), 8" (20.3 cm) and 12" (30.5 cm) tiles.

If you don't have any ceramic tiles, you can bake your clay on a cookie sheet. An airlock cookie sheet is better than a regular one.

If all you have is a regular cookie sheet, invert a second sheet on top of the first to create your own insulated cookie sheet.

It's best if you cover whichever baking surface you use with parchment paper, aluminum foil or any paper

made to withstand the heat of the oven. This will keep the bottom of your clay from becoming shiny.

Parchment paper is best if you can find it. I bought some from my local bakery before I found a roll. Check kitchen and specialty food stores.

OVEN

To bake polymer clay, all you need is a regular home oven or toaster oven. *Do not use a microwave oven.* The temperature at which you will bake the clay depends on the type of clay you are using. I recommend baking your clay at the highest temperature recommended for your clay. If you use a toaster oven, be careful where you place your item to bake, as the top of the toaster oven can get hot enough to burn your clay, which can release toxic fumes. I personally prefer the regular oven.

OVEN THERMOMETER

Because oven temperatures vary, I recommend using an oven thermometer. Prior to baking the clay, test your oven with the thermometer to find out where to set your temperature dial to get the correct temperature for your clay.

MUST-HAVE TOOLS	TRY-TO-HAVE TOOLS	NICE-TO-HAVE TOOLS
• Craft knife	• Slicing blade	• Food processor
• Needle tools	• Clay Shaper	• Garlic press
• Chisel tools	• Pattern Cutter Set	• Klay Gun
• Pasta machine or brayer	• Stylus	• Marxit
• Ceramic tiles	• Scratch tools	• Rubber mat
• Circle template	• Brushes	• Rotary Cutter
• Scotch-Brite pad	• Clay Warmer	
	• Parchment paper	

TECHNIQUES

CONDITIONING YOUR CLAY

To condition polymer clay, knead it with your hands in any way that is comfortable for you. You can create snakes, twist it, form it into a pancake or ball, run it through your pasta machine several times, or all of the above. Do whatever is best for you.

I have found that the clay will condition faster if I alternate between making pancakes and the other techniques. The clay seems to warm more easily the thinner it is.

If you have a food processor or chopper you can dedicate to your clay, you can use it to start the conditioning. Break the clay up before putting it into the food processor, and do not allow the motor to bind. After the pieces are chopped, place them in a plastic bag to knead them back together. When the clay sticks together, remove it from the bag to finish conditioning.

I found my food processor at a year-end clearance sale for less than ten dollars. Remember, the tools you use for polymer clay cannot be used for food.

Some designers use a product called Mix Quick to help condition their polymer clay. I tend not to use it just to condition my clay; however, I do add Mix Quick to the clay when making the walls of my cottages. Without Mix Quick, if you put the walls on but don't have time to finish them right away, the cooled clay may crack when you try to texture it.

TIP

While you're working, keep any clay that needs to be conditioned in a plastic bag in the pocket of your jeans or pants. Your body heat will start the conditioning, cutting down on kneading time.

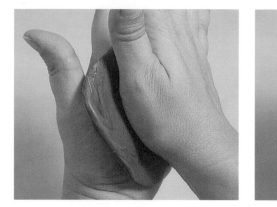

Knead the clay however feels most comfortable for you.

Rolling the clay.

Twisting the clay.

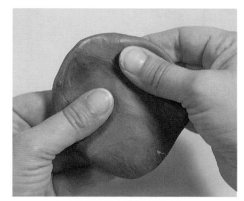

Forming clay into a pancake.

Use a food processor to make conditioning easier.

MAKING CLAY SHEETS

To create smooth sheets of clay with your pasta machine, first condition your clay and form it into a fairly thin, rectangular pancake. Run the clay through the machine starting on the no. 1 (thickest) setting. Continue to run it through the machine, increasing one number (which decreases the thickness) until the clay is as thin as you want it. The no. 6 setting is the thinnest you should go. Since all pasta machines are not the same, test the thicknesses produced by your machine against those listed on page 124. If yours are different, alter the instructions to get the equivalent thickness.

If you don't have a pasta machine and are rolling your clay with a rolling pin or brayer, see page 124 for the proper thickness.

MEASURING THE CLAY

You will need to measure your clay in order to make color mixtures and maintain consistent proportions within the projects. Polymer clay is traditionally measured with a circle template. To do this, roll your clay into a ball and place it on the template. The sizing is correct if it just fits the desired hole without being able to pass through.

If you have the new template from AMACO, you can measure your clay by placing the unconditioned block on the template and cutting it to fit the size desired. Check page 124 for additional combinations not given on the template.

If you don't have either of these templates, you can measure your clay by creating a ball and placing it on a ruler. Measure its widest point to get the size of the ball.

CREATING SNAKES

To create a snake, condition the clay and roll it first between the palms of your hands and then on a ceramic tile. To create a thinner snake, gently roll the clay with your hands, pulling outward slightly. If the snake gets too long, but is still not thin enough, cut it in two and continue to roll each section.

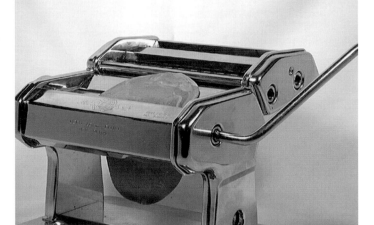

Roll smooth sheets of clay with a pasta machine.

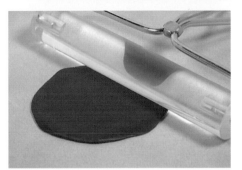

You can also use a brayer or rolling pin to create flat sheets.

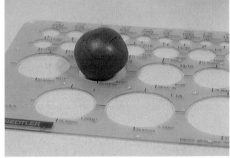

Measuring with a circle template.

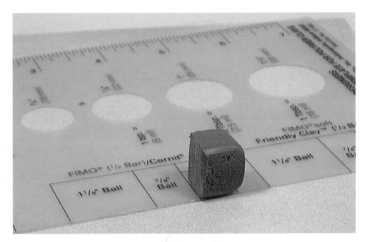

Measuring with AMACO's new template.

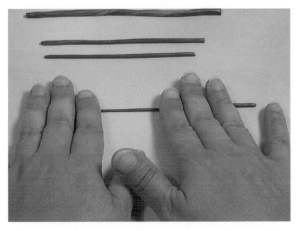

Forming snakes.

USING A KLAY GUN

I have found that the easiest way for me to use the Klay Gun is to fill it with polymer clay and then put it into my heated Clay Warmer for ten to fifteen minutes. After the gun is warm, I place the pusher on a table top covered with a rubber mat (so it won't slip). Covering the handles of the gun with a towel, I press down, allowing my weight to help push the clay through the gun.

There is also a Clay Extruder on the market. It fits on the handles of your Klay Gun and on the pusher. When a dial is turned, it extrudes the clay. See pages 124–125 for suppliers.

BAKING YOUR CLAY

You will bake your cottages in stages. The baking process will warm the previously hardened clay and bond it to the new clay. Each baking is for one hour, except the last baking, which is for two hours. For some steps, this may be longer than necessary, but it's easier to remember than many different baking times.

With the exception of Sculpey III, in my experience there is no maximum time limit for baking polymer clay. Sculpey III will scorch if baked too long. If you use this clay, do some testing first to find the maximum length of time it can be baked without scorching.

Remember to check the clay you are using for the recommended baking temperature. Do not exceed this temperature, as polymer clay will burn if baked at too high a temperature, releasing toxic fumes. Should this happen, turn off the oven, open some windows and leave the house for a while. Polymer clay does produce an odor when it is baked under normal conditions, but this is not harmful. You will be able to tell the difference in odor should you burn it.

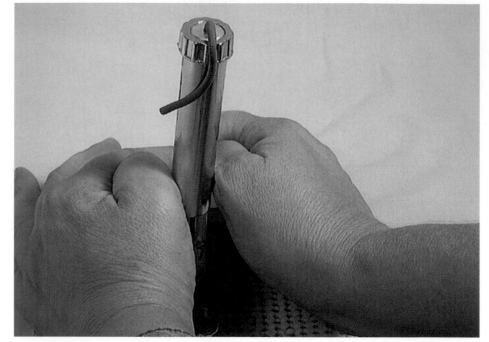

Using a Klay Gun.

Place a washer in your Klay Gun between the disc and the tube to protect the disc. I broke a disc before I got in the habit of doing this. You may have to go to the hardware store to find a washer that fits inside the Klay Gun and has a larger hole than the disc.

DON'T MISS A BAKING

As you work on your cottages, please be sure to read all the instructions for each step carefully. The cottages are baked in stages to make it easier to add each step that follows. Instructions to bake are often given at the end of a step. You don't want to overlook a baking!

TIPS ON USING POLYMER CLAY

- Anytime you are cutting with a knife, be sure to protect your surface by cutting on a ceramic tile or cutting board.

- Never work directly on a wooden surface, such as a kitchen table; polymer clays will damage the finish.

- Be careful not to leave a pattern print-side-down on the clay, as the ink will transfer to the clay.

- Keep hands and surfaces clean. Wash your hands between colors, because some pigments may stay on your hands and transfer to the next color you pick up. Be especially careful when working with white or light colors.

- I've found that hand lotion helps condition polymer clay. Test yours on some extra clay before using it on a cottage—one lotion I tried made the clay sticky.

- If you have difficulty pushing clay through your Klay Gun, add Mix Quick. Just be careful not to add too much.

- Use an old toothbrush to clean the inside of your Klay Gun.

- Since there is no exact way to measure polymer clay, your mixed colors may differ just slightly from mine. Also, the printed colors you see in this book won't match the actual clay colors exactly, so the color you are working with will probably not match mine. Don't worry! This will make your cottages unique.

- Feel free to customize your cottages to suit your tastes. Experimenting with colors is great fun. Just be sure to write down what colors you used, and in what proportions. Otherwise, it might be difficult to create the same color again.

- If you want to coat your cottages with a sealer, use one created for use with polymer clay, such as FIMO Matt or Gloss Varnish. Some of the other finishes not designed for polymer clay will make the clay sticky after a short period of time.

- If you want to make your cottages a different size, reduce or enlarge the patterns when you copy them. If you will be displaying your cottages together, use the same percent of enlargement or reduction for all your cottages so they will be in scale. If you enlarge the patterns, you will need to use more clay than instructed in the project mixtures.

- Don't leave polymer clay in a hot place, such as in your car in the summer. It will start to harden.

- If you have some clay that is crumbly, you can condition it with Mix Quick or save it in your excess clay bag. If mixed with a soft clay, it will soften up. This may take a little more time than usual. Never discard any clay. It can always be used as a base for your cottages.

- It's helpful to pick up and place small pieces, such as roof tiles and leaves, using your stylus or needle tools.

- When you're working on the brick detail, if you have trouble getting into an area, try holding your cottage in your hand and turning it upside down.

- If there is a corner or window that doesn't look right on your cottage, don't worry. Cover it with a shrub or vine and no one will ever know.

- Look around your house for items that can be used to impress texture into polymer clay. Doors can be impressed with something to give them more interest.

- You can sign your cottage by putting your initials in the grass at the back, near the edge of the base.

- Most of the village finishers—such as trees, bushes, benches, etc.—require multiple bakings. When one of your cottages is in the oven and you have some spare time, you may want to work on the extras.

- If flowers or leaves fall off after the last baking, glue them back on using white craft glue. Do not use a hot glue gun. If you want to hold something like a pin back to your clay, use Pic Stic Medium. The other glue I use frequently is Aleene's Thick Designer Tacky Glue. The white glues can be put in the oven, if needed. If you are using a different glue, care must be taken when it is baked. Test it first to be sure that it does not burn.

- Polymer clay darkens somewhat when baked.

- After it is done baking, polymer clay should be left in your oven to cool. While my clay is cooling in the oven, I turn off the oven dial but leave the temperature dial set. That way I know that there is clay in the oven and don't turn the oven on again to preheat it for something else without removing the baked clay. If your oven doesn't have separate dials for temperature and baking, tape a note to the oven door or dial to remind yourself there is a cottage in there.

- Polymer clay hardens as it cools. Because of the thickness of your cottages, it will take several hours to finish curing.

- Use only glass beads on your cottages, not plastic beads. The plastic beads may melt in the oven, ruining your creation. If you can't find the petite glass beads, or don't want to use them, you can make very small balls of clay and prebake them. To make them shine after your final baking, coat them with a clay varnish, using a very small brush.

- Do not use pre-stick felt on the base of your cottages. The type of glue on it reacts with the clay and makes it sticky.

chapter three

Basic Construction

This chapter will give you an overview of how a cottage is assembled. All the projects in this book begin with the same basic steps shown here, whether you are making a manor house, store, church or lighthouse. After you've familiarized yourself with the basic techniques in this chapter, follow the step-by-step instructions for the project you want to create. In the beginning, you may need to refer back to this chapter often for more specific instructions.

In some cases, I will give you a couple of options to accomplish a particular technique or area. I may prefer one way that is not as easy for you to do. Experiment to find your preferred method, which may be one of the ways that I do things, or a new way I haven't thought of. As long as the final results are what you want, there is no right way.

In each chapter, you will find patterns for the cottage walls and roof sections, as well as for the window and door layouts. Copy the pattern for your cottage by using a copy machine or by tracing the pattern onto a piece of tracing paper. Be sure to mark your pattern pieces with the project name, the name of the piece and the number of each piece you'll need to cut. Cut out the wall and roof patterns. Put the rest aside until needed.

You can use any color of clay for the base and cottage wall foundation. These will be covered with the wall color of the cottage you are working on. For the smaller cottages, one to two blocks of clay will be more than sufficient to form

the base. For the larger cottages, more than two blocks, or the equivalent, will be needed. After you start making the cottages, you will get a feel for the amount of clay needed.

Never discard any unused mixed clay. If the color is to be used elsewhere on the cottage or the same color is used in other cottages, it will be noted in the instructions. If not, get yourself a plastic bag or covered glass container to keep the clay in. It can be used for the foundation walls and base of your cottages.

TIP

In most or all cases, the amount of clay called for in the project instructions will be more than is needed to complete the project. This is necessary to allow for excess clay, which will be trimmed away when cutting pattern pieces out of a sheet of clay. Anytime the clay color used is not a mixture, I will not give the amount needed. If you condition too much, the clay can go in a plastic bag to be used later.

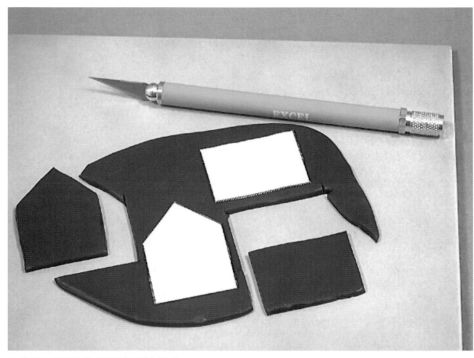

1 THE FOUNDATION WALLS

Condition any color of clay and form a pancake. Roll the clay through the pasta machine on the no. 1 setting, or, if using a rolling pin or brayer, roll to a thickness of $\frac{3}{16}$" (.5 cm). Lay the pattern pieces on the clay. Using a craft knife or kitchen knife, cut around each wall piece. (A slicing blade can also be used to cut the pieces if you have one.) If more than one wall piece is indicated, after cutting the first piece, reposition the pattern and cut the additional pieces. If you can't cut all the necessary pieces from one pancake, remove the excess clay, recondition it and run it through your pasta machine again. Repeat until all the pieces have been cut.

2 The pieces that have a red edge on the pattern need to be pressed to a 45-degree angle for a better fit. Use your chisel tool and press the edge down.

3 When an edge is pressed to 45 degrees, it tends to go out of shape. Use the chisel tool to straighten the edge.

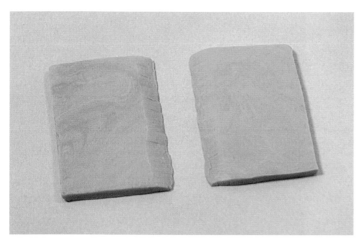

4 THE ROOF
Mix and condition the colors of clay needed for the roof foundation of the cottage you are working on. Cut the roof pieces and press the edges as you did for the foundation wall pieces.

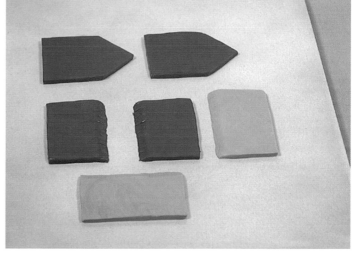

5 THE FIRST BAKING
Place the wall and roof pieces on a ceramic tile covered with parchment paper. Place another piece of parchment on top of the pieces.

6 Placing another ceramic tile on top of your wall and roof pieces keeps everything flat and prevents air bubbles from forming during baking. Preheat your oven to the recommended temperature for the clay you are using. Bake for one hour. Turn off your oven and allow the clay to cool.

TIP
The instructions will frequently tell you to place the clay on a ceramic tile covered with parchment paper. I did not show this in the pictures because the white of the parchment paper didn't show up against the white of the tile. Follow the instructions.

7 THE COTTAGE FOUNDATION

Condition any color of clay for your cottage base. Form it into a pancake approximately ¼" (.6 cm) thick and at least as large as stated in the instructions for the cottage you are working on. Place it on a ceramic tile. Press the prebaked front wall of your cottage into the base, with the flat edge down. Place the wall approximately in the center of your base, making sure there is enough room for your front yard. Position the tapered top edge as shown.

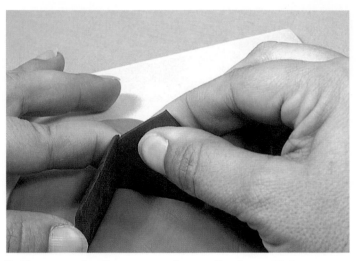

8 Place one end wall next to your front wall to form a 90-degree angle. The edge of the end wall should butt up to the back of the front wall as shown. Press the end wall into your foundation so that the top of the front wall and the start of the peak meet.

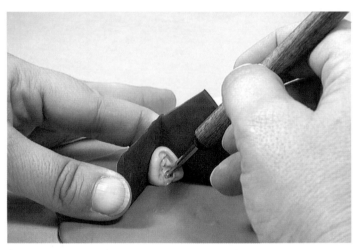

9 To anchor the walls, place a small amount of clay inside the corner you have just formed. Hold the outside edges of your walls in place, and use a paint brush handle, stylus or similar tool to press the clay into the corner. Add the back wall parallel to your front wall. Place an anchor in the new corner.

10 Slide your last end wall into the space created by your front and back walls. Press it into the base. Be sure the top edges of your front and back walls match the end walls so that your roof will fit.

11 Place a small amount of clay into the last two corners to anchor them.

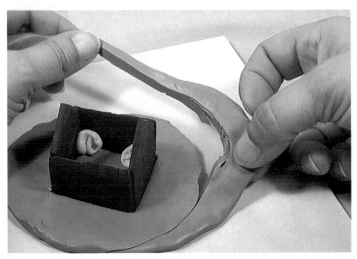

12 If your base is too large, use a craft or kitchen knife to trim it to the size indicated in the individual instructions. Remove the excess clay you've cut away and save it for the next cottage base and foundation.

13 Press around the trimmed edges so that you have a tapered base.

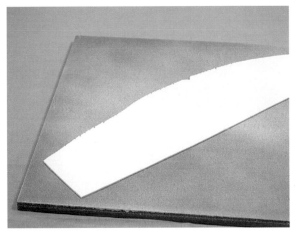

15 Condition and mix the under color clay. Roll it to the no. 5 setting on your pasta machine. Lay the sheet of clay on a ceramic tile and cut two straight edges at a 90-degree angle.

14 THE UNDER COLOR

The under color will show through the windows of your cottage. I prefer to have lit windows in my cottages, so I use a mixture of half Yellow and half White clay. You can also use Black for your under color if you want the lights to appear to be off. If you are only going to make one cottage, one-fourth of a block of Yellow and one-fourth of a block of White clay should be plenty. This mixture is used for all the cottages, so save the extra in a plastic bag marked "Under Color."

16 Starting at one edge of the front wall, wrap the under color snugly around your cottage.

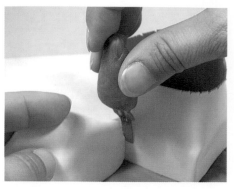

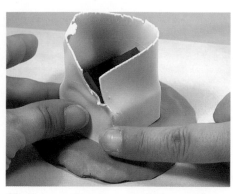

17 Using your chisel tool or craft knife, trim the excess under color where the ends meet at the front wall.

18 Use your finger to smooth the cut edge where the two ends of the under color join.

19 Press the under color over the top of the front wall.

TIP

If the under color will not go completely around your cottage, trim it at the edge of the last wall it completely covered. Recondition the excess under color that you cut away and put it through your pasta machine again. Cut a 90-degree angle the same as before and continue to cover your cottage. Trim the excess under color.

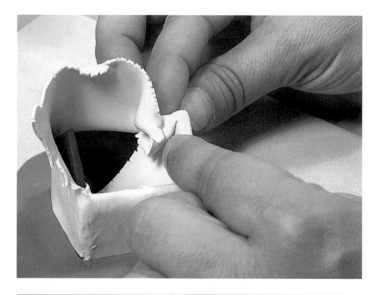

20 Press the under color along the remaining wall tops.

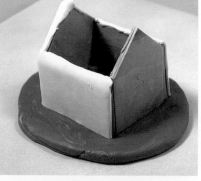

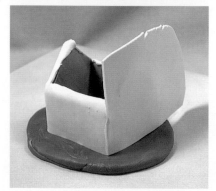

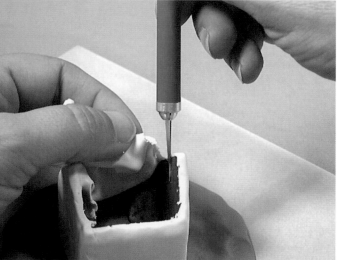

21 Trim away the excess under color along the inside of your cottage walls and smooth the under color so that there are no air bubbles on your walls.

FINISHING THE UNDER COLOR

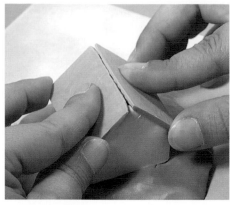

22 THE ROOF

Place the prebaked roof on your cottage with the tapered edges joining at the peak of the roof. Bake the base and assembled foundation for one hour. Cool completely for several hours before continuing so the roof can set as firmly as possible.

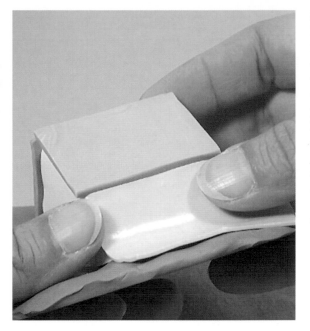

23 THE OUTER WALLS

Run the outer wall clay mixture for the cottage you are working on through your pasta machine, working up to the no. 5 setting. Cut a piece slightly larger than your cottage front. Be sure you have a 90-degree angle. Place one straight edge of the clay on the front wall under the eaves and one straight edge even with the edge of the cottage. Press the clay firmly to the wall all the way to the base.

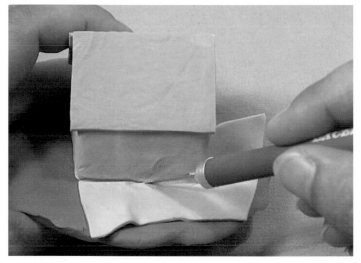

24 Using your craft knife or chisel tool, trim off the excess clay at the cottage base and at the edge of the front wall.

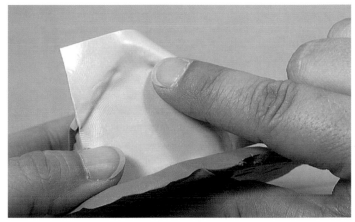

25 Cut a piece of wall color slightly larger than one end wall. Place the piece over the end wall, matching the edges to one side of the front wall and the base. Press the clay onto the wall completely up to the eaves.

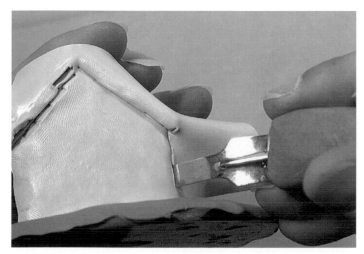

26 Use your craft knife or chisel tool to trim the excess clay at the eaves. Be careful not to cut too low. The wall needs to be close under the eaves. Also trim the excess at the edge of your end wall.

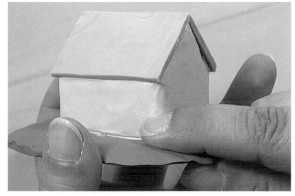

27 Press the walls firmly to your cottage, being sure there are no air bubbles. Continue to go around your cottage until all the walls are completely covered. If you need to, recondition the excess clay and run it through your pasta machine again. Smooth the joined edges with your finger until the separation is no longer visible.

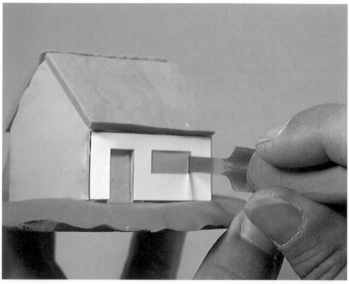

28 THE WINDOW AND DOOR OPENINGS

Photocopy or trace and cut out the pattern for the window and door openings of the cottage you are working on. Use your craft knife to cut the window and door openings out of the pattern. Place the front wall pattern on the front of your cottage, with the top edge lined up with your eaves. If the pattern is too large, trim it slightly. If it is too narrow, center it on the wall, being careful to keep the top of the pattern against the eaves. There are several different ways you can cut out the openings, depending on the stiffness of the clay you are using. If you are using a stiffer clay, you can cut out the window and door openings with your craft knife. You can also use your chisel tool. If you are using one of the softer clays, use your needle tool to mark the openings.

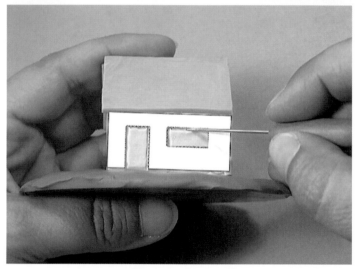

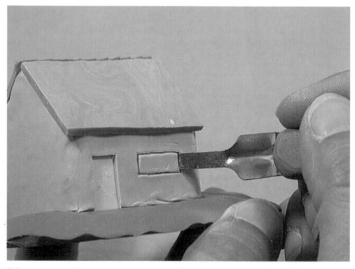

29 Remove the pattern. Use your chisel tool to cut along the marked lines, and then remove the clay with your chisel tool or craft knife.

30 Position the end wall piece on the right side of your cottage. Match the window tops on the side wall with the window tops of the front windows. If needed, trim or fold up the pattern. Continue until all the windows and doors have been cut. Follow the instructions for the cottage you are working on to texture the walls and add the chimney and sidewalks, if called for. Bake for one hour.

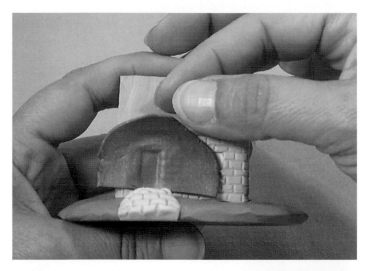

After your cottage has cooled from baking, run the door clay color through your pasta machine until you reach the no. 5 setting. Trim one edge straight. Place the straight edge along the bottom of the door opening and press it into the door opening.

32 Remove the door clay and place it on a ceramic tile with the back side up. Use your craft knife to cut the door out along the impression lines.

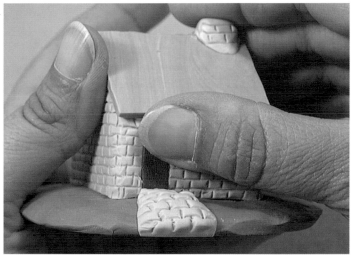

33 Press the door back into the door opening on your cottage. Make sure it completely covers the door opening.

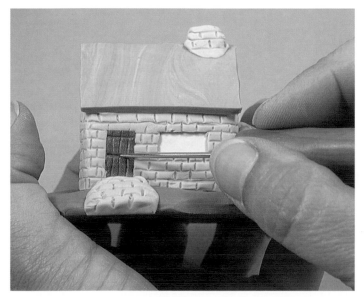

34 Follow the instructions for the cottage you are working on to texture your door.

35 Pick up a petite glass bead with your needle tool and place it on your door for a door handle.

ADDING THE DOOR

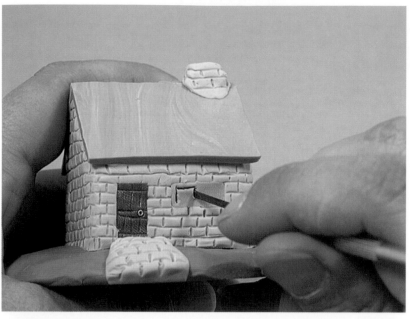

36 THE WINDOW FRAMES

Impress and cut the window frames the same way you did the door. With a fine screwdriver, cut the window pane openings.

37 Remove the cut portion from your windows, and straighten the window frames with the screwdriver. Finish all the windows in this manner.

OPTIONAL METHOD

If you have a steady hand or a slicing blade, another way to do the windows is to cut narrow strips of the window clay color. Cut two pieces the width of your windows and place them in the window at the top and bottom. Cut two pieces the height of the windows, minus the top and bottom trim, and place them in the sides of your windows. If there are crosspieces, cut and place them in the same way. Be sure to smooth the trim clay. You can also cut one strip and wrap it around the entire window opening, trimming the excess where the two ends meet.

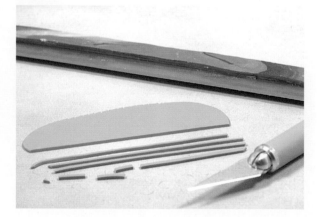

38 THE GRASS

For your grass, mix a 1" (2.5 cm) ball of White, a 1" (2.5 cm) ball of Leaf Green and a ¾" (1.9 cm) ball each of Yellow, Ochre and Bronze clay. This grass color will be used for all the cottages. The color is lighter and duller than real grass because if a true grass color is used, the grass draws attention away from the cottage.

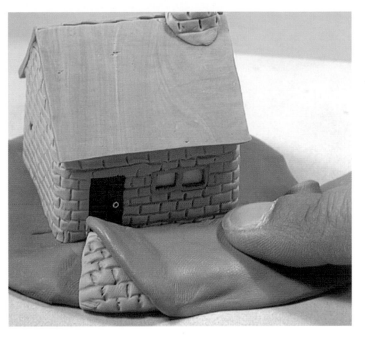

39 Flatten the grass mixture to a pancake approximately ⅛" (.3 cm) thick. You can run this through your pasta machine to the no. 3 setting, if desired. Cut the pancake in half lengthwise. Place the cut edge along the front wall of the house, overlapping the sidewalk slightly. Press it to the base, the sidewalk and the front of your cottage. Trim the excess along the edge of your sidewalk.

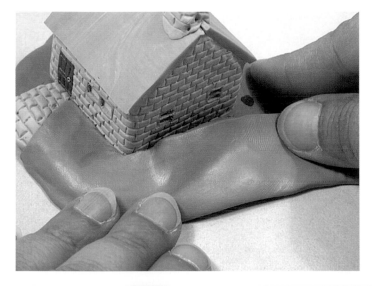

40 Stretch the grass around the corner. Press it to the base and along the wall. Continue around your cottage until the base is completely covered. If necessary, use the second half of your grass mix. Be sure to press the clay where the grass pieces meet so there isn't a lump in your grass.

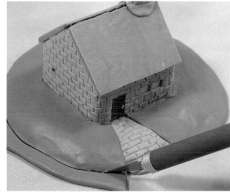

41 Trim the grass along the other edge of the sidewalk and along the base of your cottage.

42 With the wire tools, texture the grass. If you don't have a wire tool, you can make one as described on page 8, or you can texture the grass with your needle tools. This will take longer, but it works just as well.

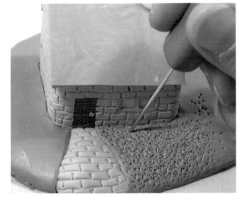

43 Use your needle tools to texture the grass where the wire tools won't reach—usually along the walls of your cottage, the sidewalk and the edge of the grass. Next, follow the instructions for the cottage you are working on to finish and bake the roof.

The cottages each have several different leaf colors. The same colors will be used for all the cottages, so remember to save them in a bag with the colors marked. After conditioning the leaf mixture needed, run it through your pasta machine to the no. 6 setting, or to approximately ½₂" (.1 cm) thickness. Place it on a piece of parchment paper.

Leaf Green

The first leaf color used is just a ⅞" (2.2 cm) ball (or the equivalent block if using an AMACO template) of Leaf Green.

Light Green

Mix a ½" (1.3 cm) ball of Green and a ⅝" (1.6 cm) ball of Golden Yellow clay.

Medium Green

Mix a ½" (1.3 cm) ball of Green, a ⅝" (1.6 cm) ball of Yellow and a ½" (1.3 cm) ball of Navy Blue clay to get a medium green.

Dark Green With Shine

You can use either or both of the dark green mixes on your cottages. This mix has a little shine to it, which I sometimes like to use. Mix a ⅝" (1.6 cm) ball each of Black, Leaf Green, Fir Green and Anthracite clay. Always use FIMO Anthracite; FIMO Soft Anthracite contains glitter.

The Other Dark Green

Mix a ½" (1.3 cm) ball of Black, a ½" (1.3 cm) ball of Green, a ⅝" (1.6 cm) ball of Yellow and a ⅝" (1.6 cm) ball of Navy Blue clay for the second dark green.

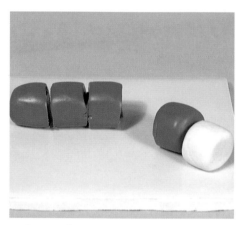

Lighter Value Leaves

After you have mixed the leaf colors, cut each mixture into four pieces. Add an equal amount of White or Yellow clay to one-fourth of each mixture. With some of the leaf colors, adding White will give you a blue-green color you may not like. This lighter version of the leaf mixture can be used to add a little variety in your foliage.

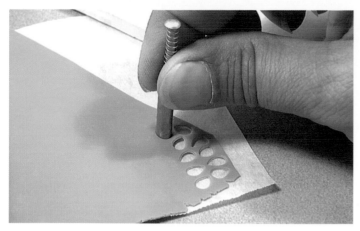

45 Follow these instructions if you have a Kemper Pattern Cutter set to make the leaves and flowers. If not, follow the instructions below. Use the teardrop- or heart-shaped pattern cutter to cut out a leaf.

MAKING LEAVES WITHOUT A PATTERN CUTTER

Roll a piece of the leaf clay into a narrow snake approximately ⅛" (.3 cm) in diameter. Cut a narrow piece and roll it into a ball in your hand.

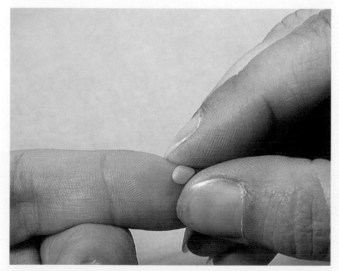

Shape the clay into a teardrop and place it on a ceramic tile. If you are doing heart leaves, press the round end with your needle tool to create a heart shape.

46 Place the cut leaf on a ceramic tile without parchment paper. If it turns upside down, use your needle tool to turn it right side up. The cutters leave a slightly rough edge and it is better not to have that on the top of your leaf. Press the leaf down on the tile so that it will not move when you create the veins.

47 THE LEAF VEINS

With your sharp needle tool, draw a vein line down the center of your leaf from the round edge to the peak. Next, draw the small veins from the center vein to the edge of your leaf.

48 To create the veins in a heart-shaped leaf, draw a center vein and then veins from the center vein out to the edge. Angle the veins slightly toward the point of the leaf.

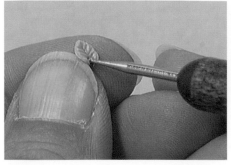

49 Use your chisel tool or sharp needle tool to pick up the leaves. Hold each leaf between your fingers and press the edges up slightly. This will give more dimension to your bushes.

50 Using a stylus or dull needle tool, place the leaf on the bushes or vines.

51 Press the leaf with your finger or Clay Shaper tool so that it is firmly attached. I learned this the hard way; I would knock off leaves that were not firmly attached, even after baking. Should this happen after your final baking, use a little white craft glue to put the leaves back on.

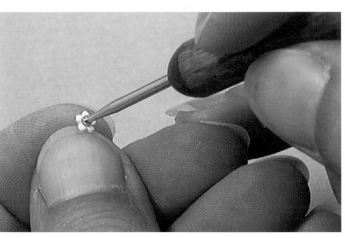

52 Run your flower color to the no. 6 setting on your pasta machine. Cut the flowers using the pattern cutter. With a stylus held in the center of your flower, press the petals up slightly.

53 Place the flowers on your bushes where indicated. Use your Clay Shaper tool to press each firmly in place.

TIP
While my cottages are baking, I fill a 4" (10.2 cm) ceramic tile with leaves to be used later. I use one tile for each color combination.

54 If your flowers have a petite glass bead center, pick up a bead with your needle tool and place it in the center of your flower. Press it firmly in place. If you dampen the tip of your needle tool, it will pick up the glass bead easily.

55 THE FELT BOTTOM

Place your cottage on a piece of Hunter Green or Black felt. Trace around the base with a marker or pen. Cut the felt slightly inside the line. Be sure it fits the base without showing.

56 Using a good white craft glue such as Aleene's Thick Designer Tacky Glue, put glue on the bottom of your cottage base. I use my finger to spread it around.

57 Put the felt on the bottom of your cottage and press firmly. Place your cottage on a piece of plastic wrap or tin foil until the glue is dry.

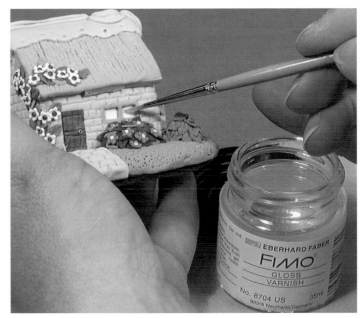

58 THE WINDOW GLOW

To give your windows a gloss that looks like glass, use a fine, round paintbrush and coat only the windows with FIMO Gloss Varnish. If you have the small bottle of varnish that has a brush included, set the brush aside and use the finer paintbrush.

chapter four

Easy Cottages

Sunny Cottage

Sunny Cottage is a charming brick cottage with a thatched roof. It would look right at home sitting beside a stream in the woods.

   Sunny Cottage is one of the easiest cottages to make. I used it as an example of basic construction in chapter three because it doesn't have any special elements to worry about. This is a good first cottage with which to begin your village.

MATERIALS

Polymer clay
- Anthracite
- Black
- Bordeaux Red
- Bronze
- Dove Gray
- Fir Green
- Golden Yellow
- Green
- Leaf Green
- Navy Blue
- Ochre
- Rosewood
- White
- Yellow

Mix Quick

Petite glass beads
- Ginger 42028
- Rainbow 40374
- Victorian Copper 42030

The must-have tools listed on page 9

Rotary cutter with a Victorian-edged blade, decorative-edged scissors or pastry cutter

Hunter Green felt

White craft glue

FIMO Gloss Varnish (optional)

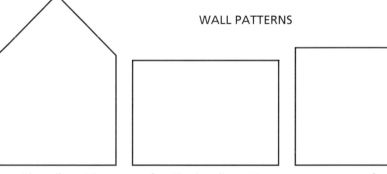

WALL PATTERNS

side walls–cut 2   front/back walls–cut 2   roof–cut 2

DOOR & WINDOW PATTERNS

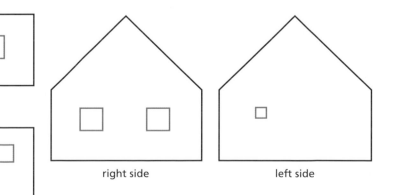

front wall

right side   left side

back wall

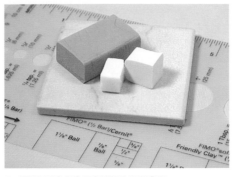

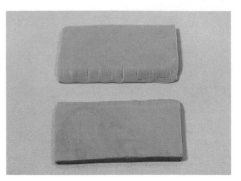

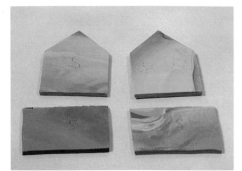

1 THE FOUNDATION WALLS

Following steps 1 and 2 of the basic instructions on pages 14-15, cut one front wall, one back wall and two end walls using the patterns on page 29. Press edges as instructed.

2 THE ROOF FOUNDATION

Mix a 1¼" (3.2 cm) ball of White and a ¾" (1.9 cm) ball of Ochre clay for the roof and roof foundation (equivalent block sizes shown here). After the roof foundation is cut, add a ⅝" (1.6 cm) ball of Mix Quick to the rest of the roof clay for the thatched roof.

3 Cut two roof pieces and press and straighten the tops as instructed on pages 14-15.

4 Place all the cut pieces on a ceramic tile and bake for one hour.

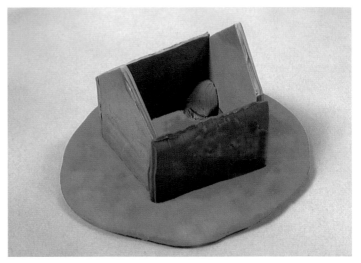

5 THE BASE AND FOUNDATION

Use scrap clay to make a pancake approximately 3½" x 4" (8.9 cm x 10.2 cm) and place it on a ceramic tile. Position the walls in the pancake base as instructed on pages 16-17.

6 THE UNDER COLOR

Cover the walls with the under color as shown on pages 17-18.

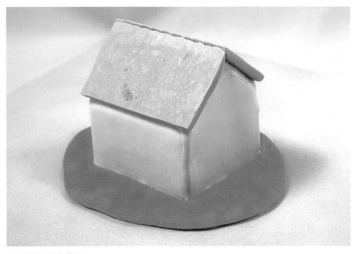

7 THE ROOF

Place the roof on Sunny Cottage (step 22, page 19) and bake for one hour. Allow to cool completely.

8 THE OUTER WALLS

Mix a ⅞" (2.2 cm) ball of White, a ⅞" (2.2 cm) ball of Ochre and a ⅝" (1.6 cm) ball of Mix Quick for the walls, chimney, sidewalk and the peak of the thatched roof. This photo shows the clay measured with two different templates. Follow the basic instructions on pages 19-20 to apply your wall clay and to cut out the door and window openings.

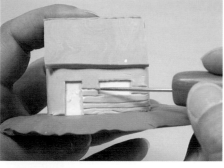

9 THE BRICKS

Using your needle tool, draw horizontal lines in the front wall, trying to stay parallel to the window bottom. Make them approximately ⅛" (.3 cm) apart or slightly less. They do not need to be completely straight and exact; the variation will give your cottage more interest.

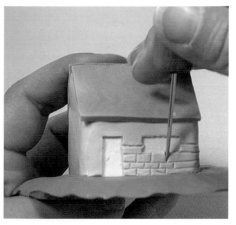

10 Still using your needle tool, draw two vertical lines in the bottom row of bricks. Now on the second row, draw a vertical line in between the vertical lines on the bottom row. Continue in this fashion to create your bricks.

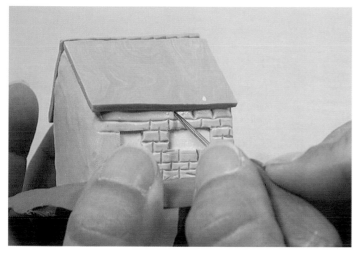

11 Carry the lines all the way to the top of the wall, under the eaves.

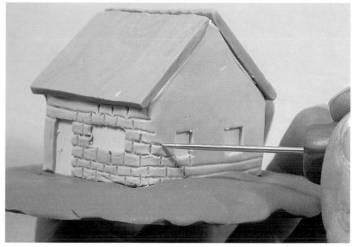

12 Using the lines on the front of Sunny Cottage as a guide, continue to draw the horizontal lines around your cottage. Because the base is not flat, the bottom line may get lost in places where the base rises slightly.

13 When you've finished the bricks, check them and, if needed, go over some again.

14 Drawing the bricks will probably stretch the window and door openings out of shape slightly. If so, press your chisel tool into the window and door openings to straighten them out.

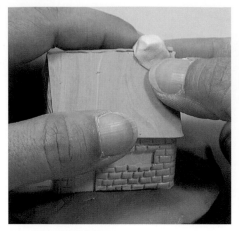

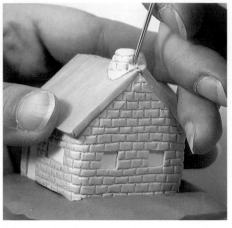

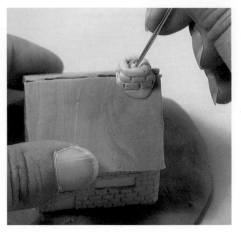

15 THE CHIMNEY
Using your wall color, add a chimney to the roof peak. Press the clay as flat as possible at the edge of the chimney where it is sitting on the roof.

16 Draw bricks on your chimney just as you did on the walls.

17 Use your needle tool to press down on the center of the chimney top.

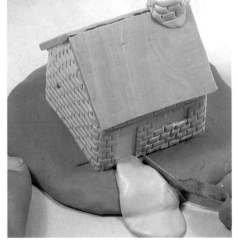

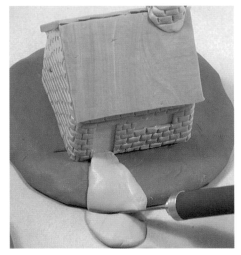

18 THE SIDEWALK
Add a sidewalk in front of the door, using the wall clay color. Press it into the door opening and keep the walk approximately ¹⁄₁₆" (.2 cm) thick.

19 Press the sidewalk along the edge of your base. Use your chisel tool to straighten out the edge of the sidewalk.

20 Trim the sidewalk at the edge of the base.

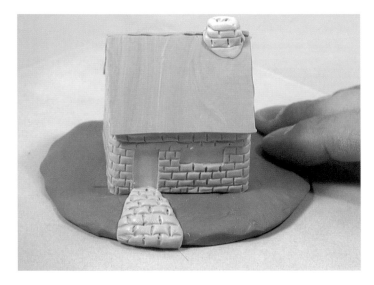

21 Make bricks in the sidewalk the same as you did in the walls and chimney. The second stage of Sunny Cottage is completed. Bake for one hour.

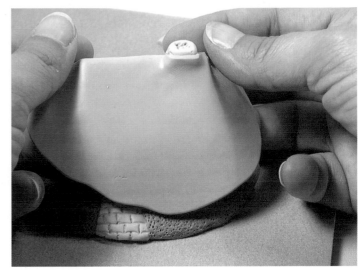

22 THE WINDOWS, DOORS AND GRASS

Follow the basic instructions on pages 21-22 to complete the door and windows. Use Dove Gray clay for the window panes and Bronze clay for your front door. To make a wooden door, draw four or five lines from the top of the door to the bottom with your needle tool. Then, draw one line near the top from side to side, two lines in the center and one line near the bottom. Add a Victorian Copper petite glass bead for your door handle.

Follow the steps on page 23 to complete the grass.

23 THE THATCHED ROOF

Run the roof mixture through your pasta machine to the no. 4 setting. Cut the clay in half. Lay one half on the roof front, placing the cut edge at the peak. Press it firmly to the roof.

24 Trim the clay at the edges of your roof and around the chimney. Complete the back of the roof in the same manner. You are now finished with this color and can put this clay mixture in your foundation bag.

25 With your scratch or needle tools, use an up-and-down stroke to scratch the clay, creating a thatched look. Use a soft brush to brush the roof clay crumbles off your roof and grass.

26 THE ROOF PEAK

Run the remainder of your wall mixture through your pasta machine to the no. 5 setting. Cut the clay in half lengthwise with your craft knife. Use a Victorian-edged rotary blade, a pair of decorative-edged scissors or a pastry cutter to cut a piece about ½" (1.3 cm) wide. If you don't have any of these tools, use your craft knife to cut a wavy line ½" (1.3 cm) wide.

27 Lay the straight edge of the piece you just cut along the peak of the cottage's roof. Do the same for the back side.

28 With your craft knife, trim this clay to a peak over the edge of the roof. Smooth the two pieces where they meet.

29 Make a snake with the remainder of the wall clay and lay it on the peak, starting at one edge, going around the chimney and down to the other edge.

30 Do the same for the back side of the roof and chimney. Lay a third snake on top of the other two and trim at the edges.

31 With your needle tool, make dot impressions along the edge. Bake for one hour.

32 THE VINES, BUSHES AND FLOWERS

I recommend you do all your vines first because, if you're like me, you'll find it easier to put on the vines if you pick up the cottage. Unfortunately, the more you handle the cottage, the more likely you are to damage any previous work.

Using Leaf Green clay and the lighter value Leaf Green mixture, create a vine with teardrop-shaped leaves (page 24) going up the left front corner. Starting on the grass, layer leaves up the wall and over the roof. Be sure to press the leaves firmly to the cottage. Place some of the leaves on top of others to create more dimension.

33 Make Yellow and White flowers and place them on the vine. Press a Ginger petite glass bead firmly into the center of each flower. If the beads are not pressed firmly, they may fall out after baking. If this happens, glue them back into place with craft glue.

34 Place a small amount of any color clay under the front window. Cover it with teardrop-shaped leaves, alternating the dark green mixture with its lighter value.

Next, place a small, flat piece of clay at the right corner of the cottage. Cover with Leaf Green heart-shaped leaves.

On the right side, put a cone-shaped piece of clay between the windows. Cover this clay with teardrop-shaped leaves using the light green mixtures.

35 Create flowers from Rosewood clay and place them on the bush under the front window. Put a tiny dot of Yellow clay in the centers of the flowers.

36 Using Bronze clay, create a log bench for the back wall. Texture it with your needle tool.

Place a small amount of any color clay in the center of the left side wall. Cover this clay with dark green heart-shaped leaves.

Use teardrop-shaped Leaf Green (including the lighter value mix) leaves to create a bush at the back left corner of the cottage.

Put Bordeaux Red flowers on the bush in the center of the left wall. Using Yellow clay, place several flowers on the bush at the back left corner. Insert a Rainbow petite glass bead in the centers of these flowers.

Bake the completed cottage for two hours. Put Hunter Green felt on the bottom and add a "glow" in the windows, if desired (see step 58 on page 27). Sunny Cottage is now finished.

Hope's Place

ope's Place is a small home with a dormer and a tile roof. This project is very easy and fun to do. You can follow my instructions exactly or personalize your own Hope's Place. Try experimenting with colors of your own design—that's part of the fun of polymer clay.

Hope's Place was the Grand Prize winner in FIMO's "Jetting to Germany" contest, professional division. This makes Hope's Place one of my favorites!

As always, some of the instructions in this chapter will refer you back to chapter three for specific instructions.

WALL PATTERNS

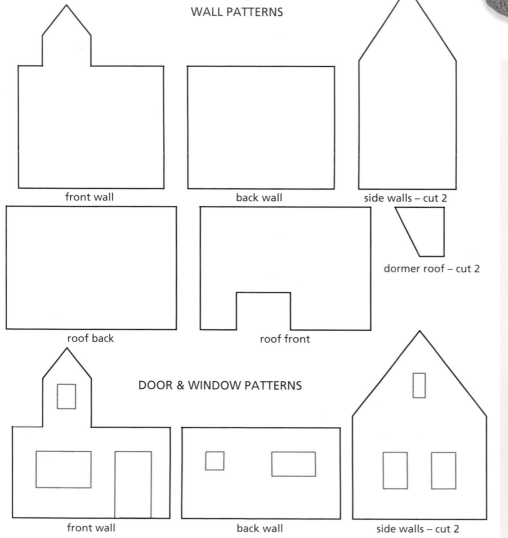

front wall

back wall

side walls – cut 2

dormer roof – cut 2

roof back

roof front

DOOR & WINDOW PATTERNS

front wall

back wall

side walls – cut 2

MATERIALS

Polymer clay
- Anthracite
- Black
- Bordeaux Red
- Bronze
- Dove Gray
- Fir Green
- Golden Yellow
- Gray
- Green
- Lavender
- Leaf Green
- Navy Blue
- Ochre
- White
- Yellow

Mix Quick

Petite glass beads
- Black 42014
- Cream 40123
- Gold 40557
- Rainbow 40374

The must-have tools listed on page 9

Hunter Green felt

White craft glue

FIMO Gloss Varnish (optional)

1 THE WALLS AND ROOF

Using the pattern on page 36 and following steps 1 and 2 of the basic instructions on pages 14–15, cut and press one front wall, one back wall and two side walls. On the front wall, press only the top of the wall, next to the dormer. The dormer is left as cut.

2 Mix a 1" (2.5 cm) ball of White and a ¾" (1.9 cm) ball of Anthracite clay until the mixture is conditioned, but still looks marbleized (the colors aren't mixed completely). Cut one roof front, one roof back and two dormer roofs.

3 Using your chisel tool at a 45-degree angle, press the cutout where the dormer will be placed. Turn the piece over.

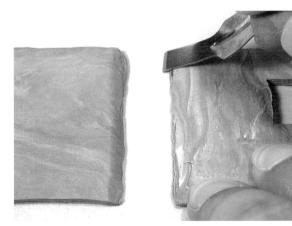

5 THE FOUNDATION

Make a pancake foundation approximately 3" x 4" (7.6 cm x 10.1 cm) and place on a ceramic tile. Place the walls in the foundation as shown (see steps 7–13, pages 16 and 17).

4 Press the peaks of the roof as instructed on page 15. Be sure you've turned over the piece with the dormer. Place the dormer roof pieces together so that the peaks that are marked in red on the pattern are touching—you will need to turn one over. Press the peak of the dormer roof. Place all the pieces on a ceramic tile and bake for one hour.

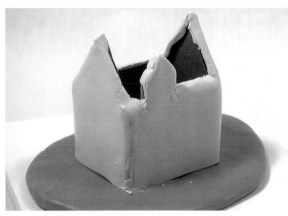

6 THE UNDER COLOR

Cover the walls with your under color as instructed on pages 17 and 18, steps 14–21. Trim the under color away from the sides of the dormer. If you don't do this, when you put the roof on, the under color will push the dormer off.

7 Take the front roof piece and slide it down the front peak of your house. If the roof front does not fit easily, place it on your ceramic tile. Use your craft knife to trim the dormer cutout slightly.

8 The roof front should fit to the dormer and peak of your house.

9 Place the back roof piece on your house.

10 Using a small piece of the under color clay, fill the dormer cutout behind the house front. This gives the dormer roof a foundation to sit on. Follow the peak of the dormer on the front wall when you do this.

11 Place your dormer roof on the cottage, matching the peaks. It's okay if the piece does not go completely to the roof front; the roof tiles will hide any gaps. Bake for one hour.

12 THE WALLS
Completely mix a 1" (2.5 cm) ball of White, a ½" (1.3 cm) ball of Gray and a ⅜" (1 cm) ball of Bronze clay for your house walls.

13 To create the front wall, run the wall color clay through your pasta machine to the no. 5 setting. Cut a piece of wall clay slightly larger than the front wall, making sure you have one 90-degree angle. Line up the 90-degree angle with the edge of one side wall and the base of your house. Using your craft knife, cut where the roof hangs over.

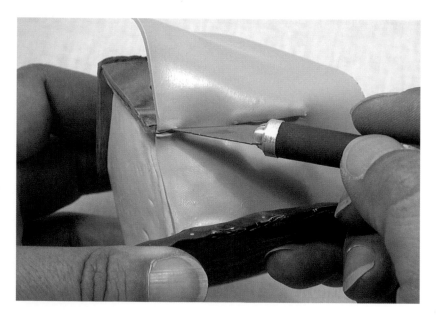

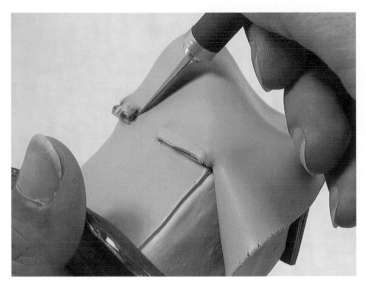

14 Cut vertically along the edge of the dormer, leaving extra clay to wrap around the side wall of the dormer.

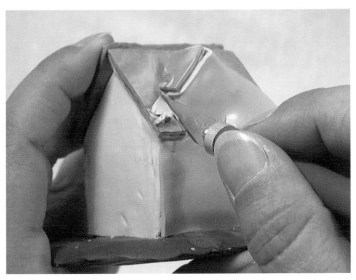

15 Press the front wall to the dormer roof, and trim away one side of the peak. Next, cut the edge of the dormer roof. Press the wall clay to the dormer side and trim away the excess. You may also have to trim under the dormer eaves. Now do the other side of the dormer roof.

16 Use your finger or Clay Shaper tool to press the front wall snugly to the base and under the eaves. Finish the remaining walls following the instructions on page 19.

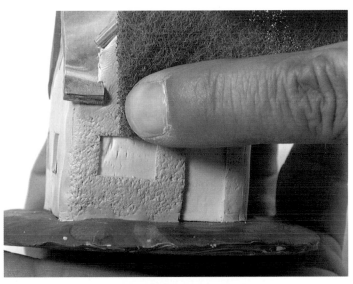

17 THE WINDOW AND DOOR OPENINGS

Cut the window and door openings as instructed on page 20. Texture all the walls with a piece of Scotch-Brite pad. After the walls are done, check that the window and door openings are still straight. If not, use your chisel tool to straighten them.

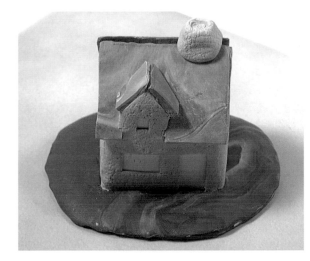

18 THE CHIMNEY

Using a small piece of wall clay, add a chimney to the right side of the roof. Press in the top of the chimney. Texture the chimney the same as you did the walls.

19 THE SIDEWALK

Add a sidewalk in front of the door following steps 18–20 on page 32. Texture the walk with the Scotch-Brite pad. Bake for one hour.

20 THE WINDOWS AND DOORS

Use a small amount of Bordeaux Red to make your door, following the instructions on page 21. Texture the door with the Scotch-Brite pad. Add a Gold petite glass bead for the doorknob. Use Dove Gray clay for the window panes (see page 22).

21 THE GRASS AND ROOF

Put grass around Hope's Place as instructed on page 23.

If you have the clay pattern cutters, run the roof clay mixture through your pasta machine to the no. 6 setting. Cut circles from the roof clay. If you don't have pattern cutters, roll a narrow snake and cut it into small pieces. Roll the pieces into balls and flatten each.

Starting at the bottom front of the roof, lay a row of circles overlapping the edge of the roof. Press the tops of the circles firmly to the roof. If needed, trim the last circle to fit. This is the hardest row to do.

22 For the second row, cut a circle in half. Lay the circle with the cut edge along the right side of the roof, overlapping the first row. Press the shingles firmly to the roof. Do the same for the left side of the roof.

23 Continue alternating rows until you reach the peak of your roof. If needed, trim the shingles next to the dormer and around the chimney.

24 Repeat this process for the dormer roof. When finished, place a circle over the edge of the peak on the dormer roof. Lay another slightly back from the first. Continue until the peak is covered.

Complete the back roof of Hope's Place the same as you did the front. When finished, place shingles at the peak just as you did for the dormer roof peak. Bake for one hour.

25 THE VINES AND BUSHES

Starting on the grass at the left corner of Hope's Place, create a vine going up the wall. Use teardrop-shaped leaves made from the medium green leaf mixture. Include some lighter leaves (see pages 24-26).

26 Continue the vine up the left side wall, over the roof, and then around the dormer window on the front and up onto the roof. Be sure to press the leaves firmly to the cottage. To create the flowers for this vine, partially mix small amounts of Bordeaux Red and White clay.

27 Put a small amount of extra clay under the front window. Cover it with teardrop-shaped Leaf Green leaves.

Next, make a cone of clay and place it at the right corner. Cover it with heart-shaped shiny dark green leaves.

Place a flat pancake of clay on the back right corner. Cover it with light green teardrop-shaped leaves, using mostly the lighter value of this mix.

28 Place White and Dove Gray flowers on the bush under the front window. Insert a Rainbow petite glass bead in the center of each flower.

Make flowers from Bordeaux Red and put them on the bush at the back right of your cottage. Use a Cream petite glass bead in each flower.

29 Put a small, cone-shaped piece of clay between the windows at the back of the cottage. Cover this bush with teardrop-shaped leaves made of Leaf Green and the lighter value Leaf Green mixture. Place some clay around the back corner and cover it with teardrop-shaped medium green leaves. For the last bush, place a small ball of clay under the right window and mold it up slightly between the windows. Add heart-shaped dark green leaves. Add Lavender flowers with Black petite glass bead centers on the bush at the back corner. Bake for two hours. Glue Hunter Green felt to the bottom of the cottage. If desired, put a glow in the windows (see step 58 on page 27). You have now completed Hope's Place.

Lambert's Home

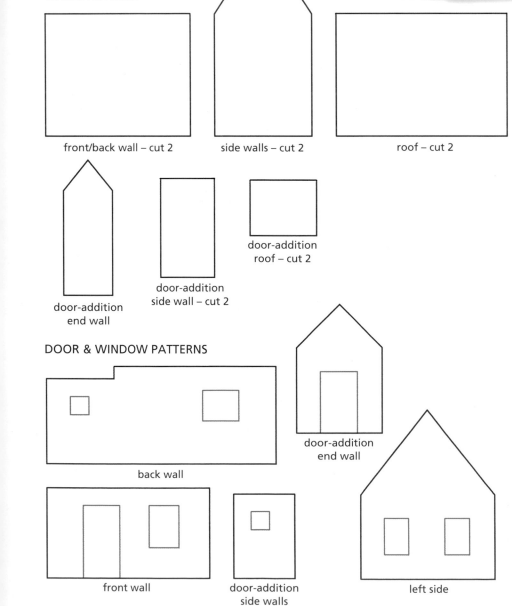

Lambert's Home is a charming, red brick home with a door addition, shutters and a connecting sidewalk. Lambert's Home is fairly simple to do, as it builds on the basic box design. The brick style and color will make it stand out in your village.

WALL PATTERNS

front/back wall – cut 2

side walls – cut 2

roof – cut 2

door-addition
end wall

door-addition
side wall – cut 2

door-addition
roof – cut 2

DOOR & WINDOW PATTERNS

back wall

door-addition
end wall

front wall

door-addition
side walls

left side

MATERIALS

Polymer clay
- Anthracite
- Black
- Bordeaux Red
- Bronze
- Dove Gray
- Fir Green
- Golden Yellow
- Gray
- Green
- Leaf Green
- Navy Blue
- Ochre
- Rosewood
- Terra Cotta
- White
- Yellow

Mix Quick

Petite glass beads
- Black 42014
- Gold 40557
- Heather Mauve 42024

The must-have tools listed on page 9

Slicing blade (optional)

Marxit (optional)

Hunter Green felt

White craft glue

FIMO Gloss Varnish (optional)

1 THE WALLS AND ROOF

Following the basic instructions in chapter three, cut one front, one back and two side walls, two door-addition side walls and one door-addition end wall from any color of clay. Use a 1⅛" (2.9 cm) ball of Anthracite clay for the roof. Cut two house roof pieces and two door-addition roof pieces. Bake for one hour.

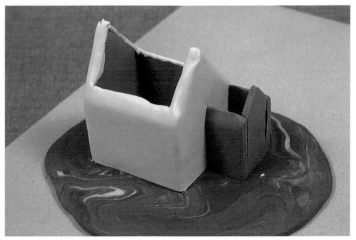

2 THE FOUNDATION AND UNDER COLOR

Make a pancake base approximately 2½" x 3½" (6.4 cm x 8.9 cm). Place the front, back and end walls in the base, following the instructions in chapter three. Cover with the under color. Now line up one door-addition side wall with the back wall and press it into the base. Add the door-addition end wall, then the other side wall.

3 Cover the door addition with the under color and add the roof pieces. Bake for one hour.

4 THE WALLS

Mix a ¾" (1.9 cm) ball each of White, Bronze and Mix Quick clay with a ⅝" (1.6 cm) ball of Bordeaux Red and a ½" (1.3 cm) ball of Terra Cotta clay for the wall color.

5 Cover the front wall as shown in chapter three. On the side with the door addition, cover the house wall first. Trim the excess clay around the door addition along the roof.

6 Next, cover the side and end walls of the door addition with the wall clay. Finish covering the other walls.

7 THE WINDOW AND DOOR OPENINGS

Cut the door and window openings on the front and right side.

8 Cut the window openings on the back and left side.

9 THE WALL TEXTURE

Follow the instructions for creating the brick texture in steps 9–14 on page 31, except place the lines closer together to create smaller bricks.

10 THE SIDEWALK

Using the wall color clay, make a sidewalk extending from each door to the edge of the base. Connect the two sidewalks with another piece of clay wider than the sidewalk, and cut out a connecting path. Smooth the sidewalks where they connect, and create the brickwork on the sidewalk the same as you did for the walls.

11 THE SHUTTERS

Roll the roof clay through the pasta machine to the no. 5 setting. Cut strips ⅛" (.3 cm) wide and the height of the windows. Carefully place these shutters on the walls next to the front window. When you have them where you want them, gently press the shutters to the walls. Using a precision screwdriver, make lines in the shutters. Also place shutters on the small window of the door addition.

12 Do the same for the back and left side windows. Bake for one hour.

13 THE WINDOWS AND DOORS

Using Gray clay, follow the basic instructions in chapter three to create the doors. Use your needle tool to add the door design. Use a Gold petite glass bead for the door handle. When there are shutters on a house, it is very difficult to press clay into the window openings. Therefore, it is best to cut strips of White clay and to make the window frames using the optional method on page 22. The front window has a horizontal and vertical cross-frame. The small window in the door addition has only an outside frame.

14 Add the frames to the larger window in the back the same as you did to the front window. The small window on the back is the same as the front door-addition window. The left side windows have only one cross-frame.

15 THE GRASS

Place a small piece of the grass mixture clay in the opening next to the cottage created by the sidewalk. Trim the grass clay to the sidewalk. Continue until all the grass is placed and then texture it, following the instructions in chapter three.

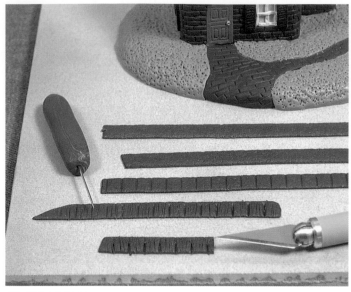

16 THE ROOF

The roof tiles are created by running the roof clay left over from step 1 through your pasta machine to the no. 5 setting. Now run the pancake you just created through the large noodle attachment of your pasta machine, or cut strips ¼" (.6 cm) wide. Texture with your Scotch-Brite pad. With your needle tool, create lines across the shingles. If you have a Marxit, press it on the strips of clay using the 5mm side, or use a ruler and mark the strips every ⅜" (1 cm). With your craft knife, cut halfway through the strips where marked.

17 Place a strip on the roof and trim it at the edge. Place the second strip on the roof, positioning the cuts on the strip between the cuts on the previous strip. Continue until the roof fronts are done, and then do the same for the back. For the roof peak, use a strip that is not marked and cut. Place it on the roof peak and trim it at the edge.

18 THE BUSHES AND FLOWERS

Use one of the dark leaf mixtures along with its lighter value (see page 24) to create a vine with teardrop-shaped leaves at the left front corner of the cottage. Carry the vine over the door at the front. On the side, carry the vine over the windows and onto the roof.

19 With White and Rosewood clay, create flowers for the vine. Place a Heather Mauve petite glass bead in the centers of the flowers.

20 Use a small amount of clay for the base of the bushes under the front window and in the corner of the door addition. Under the front window, use Leaf Green heart-shaped leaves. Also place some of these leaves in the grass on the outside of the sidewalk. Use the medium green leaf mixture in a teardrop shape for the bush in the corner.

21 Place a few Dove Gray clay flowers on the bush under the front window. Use Yellow clay for the flowers in the corner. Add a Black petite glass bead for the centers of these flowers.

22 Place a cone of clay between the windows at the back of the cottage, a piece of clay under the larger window and two small pieces of clay under the windows on the left side. Make heart-shaped leaves out of the dark green mixture and put them on the bush between the windows at the back. Use the light green leaf mixture in a teardrop shape under the back window, and heart-shaped leaves made of the medium green mixture on the bushes at the side.

23 Use Yellow clay flowers for the bush under the back window. Add a small ball of White clay for the centers.

Bake the completed cottage for two hours. When cool, cover the bottom of Lambert's Home with Hunter Green felt. If desired, put a glow in the windows as instructed in step 58 on page 27.

James' Place

James' Place is a small home with light blue siding and cement sidewalks leading to the front and back doors. It is slightly more challenging than the previous cottages; it requires patience and coordination to keep the siding straight. James' Place will add some diversity to your village.

MATERIALS

Polymer clay
- Anthracite
- Apricot
- Black
- Bronze
- Carmine
- Dove Gray
- Fir Green
- Golden Yellow
- Gray
- Green
- Leaf Green
- Midnight Blue
- Navy Blue
- Ochre
- Pearl
- White
- Yellow

Mix Quick

Petite glass beads
- Gold 40557
- Royal Blue 40020
- Royal Plum 42012
- White 40479

The must-have tools listed on page 9

Slicing blade

Marxit (optional)

Sand

Hunter Green felt

White craft glue

FIMO Gloss Varnish (optional)

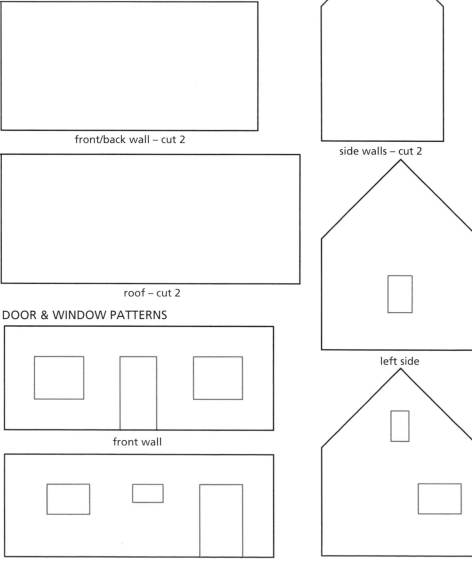

WALL PATTERNS

front/back wall – cut 2

roof – cut 2

side walls – cut 2

left side

right side

DOOR & WINDOW PATTERNS

front wall

back wall

1 THE BASE

Following the basic instructions in chapter three for all of the following steps, cut a front and back wall and two side walls. Using Midnight Blue clay, cut two roof pieces. Bake for one hour. Make a pancake base about 3½" X 4" (8.9 cm X 10.2 cm). Place the walls on the base and cover with the under color. Add the roof. Bake again for one hour.

2 THE SIDING

Mix a ⅞" (2.2 cm) ball of Dove Gray and a ⅞" (2.2 cm) ball of White clay for the siding (equivalent blocks shown here). Run through your pasta machine to the no. 6 setting.

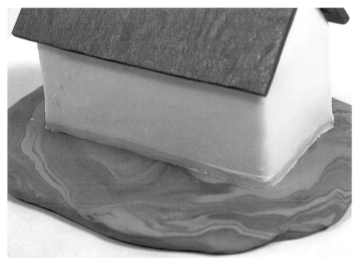

3 If you have a Marxit, use the 3mm side and mark your clay on the sides. If you do not have a Marxit, use a ruler to mark the edges. With a slicing blade, cut the pancake into strips.

4 Place one strip all the way around the house along the base. Add a second strip at the end of the first if it doesn't go all the way around. Press the top of the strip to the wall. Because the base will not be straight, this is simply to cover the bottom of the wall.

5 Take one strip of siding and place it at the edge of the front wall. Hold it out on the other edge and get it as straight as possible. When straight, press along the strip to anchor it to the wall. Now wrap it around to the side wall and position it as you did on the front wall. It's best to cut the strip at the corner of the house if it won't complete the next wall. Add another strip, matching the first, until that piece of siding is completed all the way around the house. Continue in this manner until all the siding is in place.

6 THE WINDOW AND DOOR OPENINGS AND SIDEWALK

Cut the window and door openings. It's best to use your chisel blade to cut the openings for this home—I used my craft knife on one window and pulled the siding out of place. (I've covered this with a bush. No one who sees the piece will ever know, unless they read this book!) Mix a ⅝" (1.6 cm) ball of White and a ½" (1.3 cm) ball of Gray clay for the sidewalks. Place on the base from the doors to the edge of the base. Press some sand on the sidewalks to make them look more like cement.

7 THE ROOF

Mix a ¾" (1.9 cm) ball of Black and a ¾" (1.9 cm) ball of Anthracite clay for the roof shingles. Roll through your pasta machine to the no. 5 setting. Next, run this clay through the wide noodle attachment or mark and cut ¼" (.6 cm) strips. Texture the strips with your Scotch-Brite pad, then by poking with your needle tool. Place the strips on the roof until the front and back are completely covered. Put a final strip on the peak of the roof. Allow this strip to come over the edges slightly; cut it to a peak. Bake for one hour.

8 THE WINDOWS AND DOORS

Use Midnight Blue clay for the doors and White clay for the window frames. Add a Gold petite glass bead for the door handles.

9 Cut a window in the back door. Next, put the grass on James' Place. Bake for one hour.

10 THE BUSHES AND FLOWERS

Place a cone of clay on the front corners of the house. Cover the cones with light green teardrop-shaped leaves. Place a small pancake of clay under the front windows. Cover this with heart-shaped dark green and lighter-value leaves. Make a mixture of half Carmine and half Pearl clay for the flowers on these bushes. This mixture will also be used on a bush at the back of your home. Add a White petite glass bead in the centers of these flowers.

11 Use teardrop-shaped leaves made with the dark green mixture on the back corner of the house, starting under the window on the left side and continuing around the corner and underneath the large window in back. Cover with Pearl flowers. Use a Royal Blue or a Royal Plum bead in the centers of the flowers.

12 Place some clay under the back window. Cover this with Leaf Green teardrop-shaped leaves. Use the flower clay from the front for the flowers on this bush.

Put a cone of clay at the corner next to the back door and cover it with dark green heart-shaped leaves.

13 Put a small amount of clay on the left side and cover with Leaf Green teardrop-shaped leaves, adding some leaves of the lighter value. Use Apricot clay for flowers on this bush.

Bake for two hours. Glue Hunter Green felt to the bottom. If desired, paint a glow in the windows. James' Place is now completed. Enjoy!

chapter five

Distinctive Dwellings

Pine Crest Cabin

Pine Crest Cabin, nestled in the woods bordering the village, is warm and inviting. Its cozy front porch is perfect for relaxing in the evenings.

The porch adds a bit of complexity to this house. The front door and windows are also a little more challenging than the other cottages, but the result is worth the work.

MATERIALS

Polymer clay
- Anthracite
- Apricot
- Black
- Bordeaux Red
- Bronze
- Carmel
- Champagne
- Dove Gray
- Fir Green
- Golden Yellow
- Green
- Jasper
- Leaf Green
- Navy Blue
- Ochre
- White
- Yellow

Mix Quick

Antique Gold glass bead 00221

Petite glass beads
- Black 42014
- Ginger 42028
- Victorian Gold 42011

The must-have tools listed on page 9

Klay Gun

Clay Warmer

Blush brush

Brown eye shadow

⅛" (.3 cm) wooden dowel

Hunter Green felt

White craft glue

FIMO Gloss Varnish (optional)

WALL PATTERNS

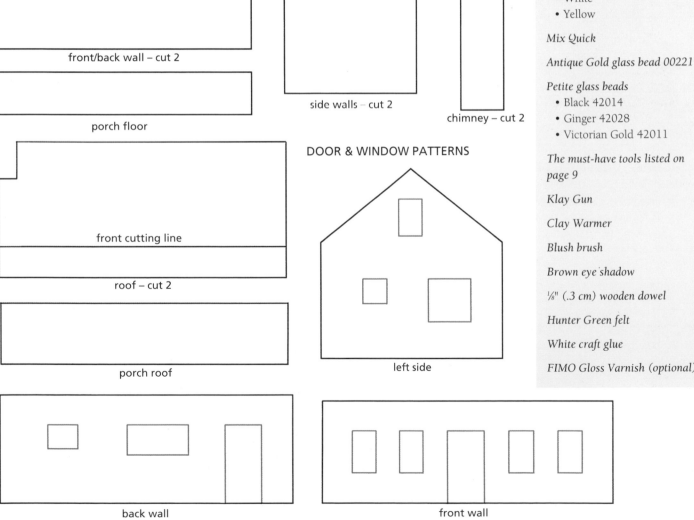

front/back wall – cut 2

porch floor

side walls – cut 2

chimney – cut 2

front cutting line

roof – cut 2

porch roof

DOOR & WINDOW PATTERNS

left side

back wall

front wall

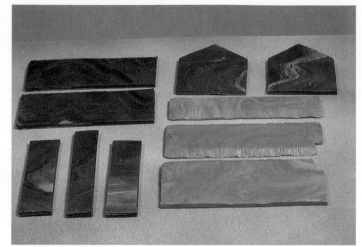

1 THE WALLS AND ROOF FOUNDATION

For the cabin roof, mix half a block of Carmel with 1⅛" (.3 cm) balls each of Golden Yellow clay, White clay and Mix Quick (equivalent blocks shown here). From this mix, cut one roof back, one roof front, one porch floor and one porch roof. Save the remainder for your logs.

2 Using any color of clay, cut two front/back walls, two side walls and two chimney pieces. Taper the front and back walls, roof tops and one side of the porch roof. The edges that should be pressed are indicated on the pattern in red. Bake for one hour.

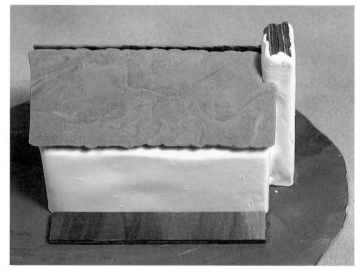

3 THE BASE, UNDER COLOR AND ROOF

Condition and roll any color clay to the no. 5 setting. Place the clay on a piece of kitchen parchment, then put the two prebaked chimney pieces on the clay. Cut around the pieces, and then place the stacked pieces in the center of one of the side walls.

4 Condition any color of clay and make a pancake approximately 4" X 5" (10. 2 cm X 12.7 cm) for the base. Place the foundation walls in the base, adding the chimney on the right. Cover the walls with the under color, and then place the roof front and back on. Put the porch floor on the base, next to the front wall.

5 THE STONES

Mix a ⅝" (1.6 cm) ball of Champagne, a ⅝" (1.6 cm) ball of Bronze and a ⅝" (1.6 cm) ball of Jasper clay just until marbleized (don't blend the colors completely). The equivalent blocks are shown here. Roll to the no. 4 setting on your pasta machine.

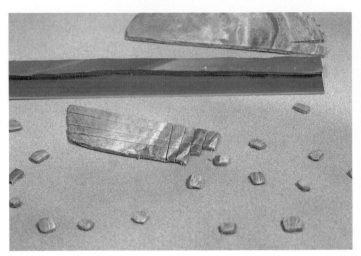

6 Place the pancake on a ceramic tile and cut into small "stones." Use a slicing blade if you have one; otherwise, you can use your craft knife. Round the corners slightly by pressing with your fingers. Bake the cabin and stones for one hour.

7 THE CHIMNEY

Run some Champagne clay through your pasta machine to the no. 4 setting and place it around your chimney.

8 Press your stones into the chimney.

9 THE WALLS

Recondition your roof base clay and put it into your Klay Gun. There are five discs with one hole included with your Klay Gun. Use the middle disc. Place a washer over the disc (see page 12). Place the Klay Gun in your Clay Warmer for ten to fifteen minutes. Press out the logs. Repeat until you have used most of the clay mixture. If you do not have a Klay Gun, roll snakes to ⅛" (.3 cm) in diameter. Place a log on the back wall, matching the wall edges. Next, place logs on the edge walls, allowing the logs to extend to the log at the back.

10 Now place a log the same size as the side wall on top of each of the first side wall logs. Next, cut a log for the front that extends to the edges of the side wall logs.

Repeat this process, alternately extending the front/back logs or the side logs every other row. Note how the ends of the longer logs fit into the recesses left by the logs that are the same size as the wall.

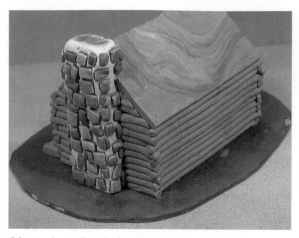

11 On the wall with the chimney, you will need to cut the logs at either side of the chimney. At the peaks of the roof, you will need to taper the logs to fit snugly against the roof edge.

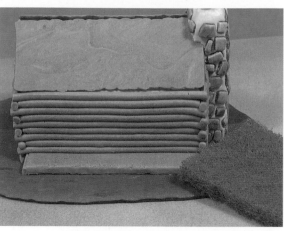

12 Using your Scotch-Brite pad, texture the logs slightly.

13 If you have several colors of brown eye shadow, pick up a mix of shadow on a blush brush. Tap the walls with the shadow to give a little color to the logs.

14 THE WINDOW AND DOOR OPENINGS

Cut the front doors and windows using your chisel blade. If the tops of the openings remove only a portion of a log, extend the cuts up to the break above that log and remove the portion. (In other words, end the openings between logs, not on a log.)

15 Match the window tops on the side to the window and door tops from the front and cut the left side windows. Now do the door and windows at the back.

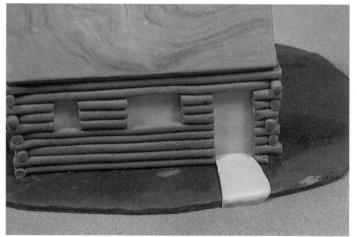

16 THE SIDEWALK

Use Champagne clay to make the walkway from the front porch to the side of the base. Also make a walkway at the back door.

17 Press stones into the walkways as you did for the chimney.

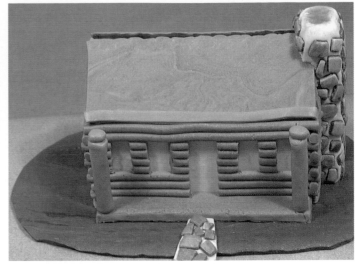

18 THE PORCH

Cut two 1" (2.5 cm) pieces from a ⅛" (.3 cm) dowel. Cover the dowel pieces with the log clay that has been run through the pasta machine to the no. 5 setting. Put a strip of clay ⅛" (.3 cm) wide along the front edge of the roof. Place a small ball of clay on top of the dowels, and put the dowels at the corners of the porch.

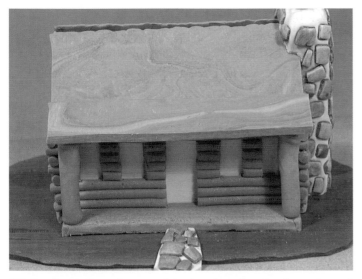

19 Put the porch roof on top of the dowels and on the clay at the roof edge. Be sure the dowels are straight. Bake for one hour.

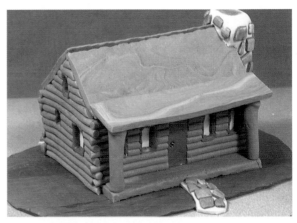

20 THE WINDOWS AND DOORS

Run Carmel clay through your pasta machine to the no. 3 setting. Carefully place the clay in the door opening on the front. Cut strips ½₂" (.1 cm) wide and place in the front windows around the edge. Use an Antique Gold glass bead for the door handle.

21 Next, do the back door and windows at the side and back of your cabin.

22 THE ROOF TILES

Mix a 1⅛" (2.9 cm) ball of Bronze, a ⅝" (1.6 cm) ball of Black and a ⅝" (1.6 cm) ball of Carmel clay (or the equivalent blocks) for the roof tiles.

23 Run the roof tile clay first through your pasta machine to the no. 5 setting and then through the large noodle attachment. Texture the strips with your Scotch-Brite pad and the sharp needle tool. Cut pieces in varying sizes from ⅛" (.3 cm) to ¼" (.6 cm) wide.

24 Place the roof tiles along the side edges of the roof, starting from the front edge and going up to the peak. Do the back edge also.

25 Starting at the front porch edge, place one row of tiles in a random pattern. Do a second row overlapping the first. With your sharp needle tool, go over the tile edges slightly to get a rougher texture. Continue up the porch roof to the cabin roof peak. Do the same thing for the back roof.

26 Cover the roof peak from the roof edge to the chimney.

27 THE GRASS

Place grass around your cabin and texture it. Bake for one hour.

28 THE TREE

Using one of the dark green leaf mixtures, create uneven circles about 1" (2.5 cm) in diameter. With your needle tools, go around the edges of your circles.

29 Place the circles on the grass on the left side of your base. Make additional circles, getting slightly smaller as you go. As you put the circles on the tree, go over the edge again with your needle tools so that they blend.

30 For the top of the tree, make a cone of clay, texture the top of the cone, and place it on top of your tree. Now blend the bottom of the cone into your tree.

31 THE BUSHES AND FLOWERS
Use Leaf Green teardrop-shaped leaves, including the lighter-value mixture, to make a vine at the left corner of your cabin. Extend the vine along the porch, up to the roof.

32 Use Bordeaux Red flowers on this vine. Place a Victorian Gold petite glass bead in the centers of the flowers.

33 Make two ¼" (.6 cm) balls of Dove Gray clay for flowerpots. Make several teardrop-shaped leaves from the grass mixture clay and place on your pot.

34 Place the pots on the porch next to the front door.
Using the light green mixture, make a small bush of heart-shaped leaves near the porch at the front of your cabin.

35 Place two pancakes of clay next to your chimney and cover them with dark green teardrop-shaped leaves. Place Apricot flowers on these bushes. Use a Ginger petite glass bead in the centers of the flowers.

36 Make several logs from Bronze clay and place them next to the back door. Texture them with your needle tools.

37 With light green teardrop-shaped leaves and Bordeaux Red flowers, make a small bush at the back of the house. Add Black petite glass beads in the centers of the flowers. Bake for two hours.

Glue a piece of Hunter Green felt on the bottom of your cabin. If desired, create a glow in the windows. Your Pine Crest Cabin is now completed.

Wellington Manor

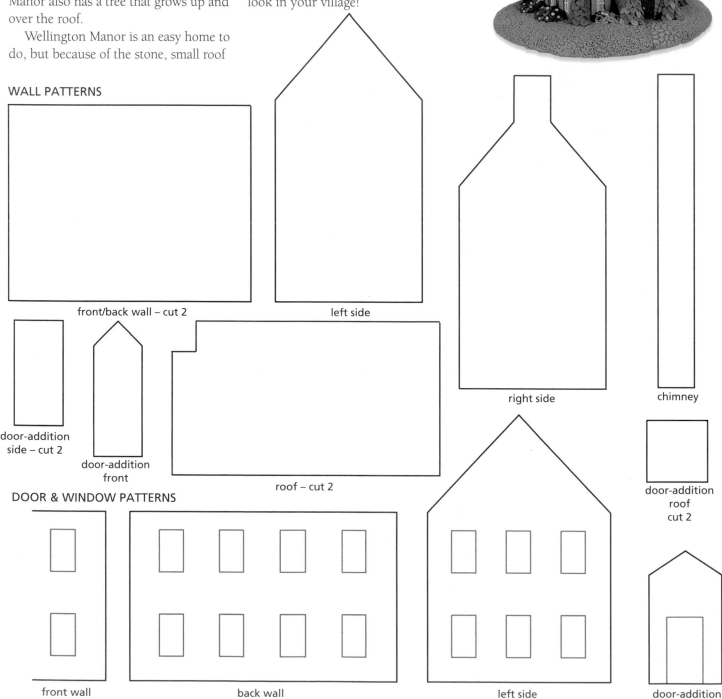

Wellington Manor is a two-story stone manor home with a front door addition. It has a detailed and interesting roof and a tall chimney on one side. At the back corner, Wellington Manor also has a tree that grows up and over the roof.

Wellington Manor is an easy home to do, but because of the stone, small roof tiles and the tree, it is one of the most time-consuming. However, I know you will love Wellington Manor so much that the time needed to do it is not important. Just think how great it will look in your village!

WALL PATTERNS

front/back wall – cut 2

left side

right side

chimney

door-addition side – cut 2

door-addition front

roof – cut 2

door-addition roof cut 2

DOOR & WINDOW PATTERNS

front wall

back wall

left side

door-addition front

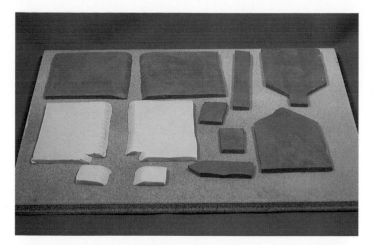

1 THE WALLS AND ROOF

Cut one front and one back wall, one side with the chimney and one side without the chimney, two door-addition sides, one door end and one chimney.

Mix a 1⅛" (2.9 cm) ball of Champagne and a 1⅛" (2.9 cm) ball of White clay for the roof base. This mixture will also be used for the window frames, so set the remainder aside. Cut two main roof pieces and two door-addition roof pieces. Lay the main roof pieces so the chimney cut-outs match. Press the chimney cut-outs to 45 degrees. Turn the pieces over and press the peak. Do the same for the door-addition peaks. The chimney cutouts will look like they are on the wrong edge. This is because the roof pieces are upside down.

Bake for one hour.

2 THE BASE AND FOUNDATION

Roll a piece of clay to the no. 5 setting on your pasta machine and put it on a piece of parchment. Place the chimney piece on the clay and cut it out. Put the chimney on the wall side that has the chimney.

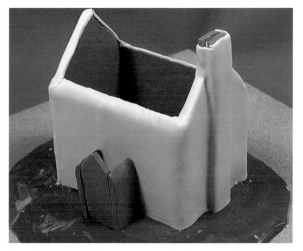

3 Make a pancake base approximately 4" x 5" (10.2 cm x 12.7 cm). Place the four major foundation walls in the base and cover them with the under color. Put in the door-addition walls, centering the addition along the front of the manor. Cover the door addition with the under color.

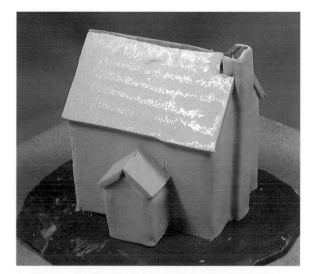

4 Place the roof pieces on the manor. Bake one hour.

MATERIALS

Polymer clay
- Anthracite
- Black
- Bordeaux Red
- Bronze
- Fir Green
- Golden Yellow
- Gray
- Green
- Jasper
- Lavender
- Leaf Green
- Midnight Blue
- Navy Blue
- Ochre
- Orange
- Terra Cotta
- White
- Yellow

Mix Quick

Petite glass beads
- Black 42014
- Old Rose 40553
- Victorian Copper 42030

The must-have tools listed on page 9

Victorian roller blade

Rotary cutter, special-edge scissors or pastry cutter

Hunter Green felt

White craft glue

FIMO Gloss Varnish (optional)

5 THE WALLS

Mix a 1" (2.5 cm) ball of White, a ⅝" (1.6 cm) ball of Bronze, a ½" (1.3 cm) ball of Gray and a ⅝" (1.6 cm) ball of Mix Quick (the equivalent blocks shown here) for the walls. Mix only until the clay is conditioned, leaving the colors marbleized. Do not mix completely. This mixture will also be used for the sidewalk.

6 Do the front wall of your house around the door addition first.

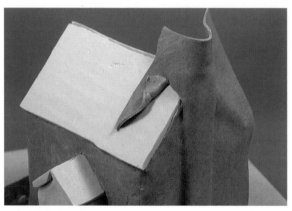

7 On the end wall with the chimney, work the wall clay around the chimney, cutting the clay at the roof and wrapping it around the chimney.

8 Trim and smooth the clay around the chimney. Impress the top of the chimney.

9 Next, put the wall clay on the door addition. Continue around Wellington Manor until all the walls are complete. Smooth the walls and edges. Save the excess wall mixture for the sidewalk.

10 THE DOOR AND WINDOW OPENINGS

Using the patterns given on page 62, cut the door opening. Cut the window openings on the right side of the front wall. Turn the pattern over to cut the left side.

11 Cut the left side windows; be sure to match the height of these windows with the front windows.

12 Cut the windows on the back side. You can trim the pattern so that the back windows match the side windows.

13 THE STONE WALLS

Press the head of an ⅛" (.3 cm) precision screwdriver into the walls in squared-off circles to create the stone look.

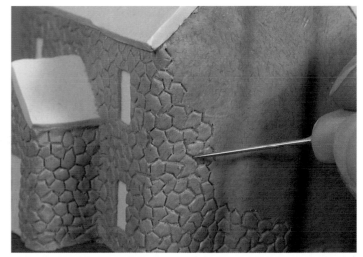

14 Smooth the stones with your needle tool. Brush the walls with a soft brush to remove any pieces of clay. You may need to go over the stones a couple of times until they are uniform in depth.

15 THE SHUTTERS

Roll Dove Gray clay through your pasta machine to the no. 5 setting. Cut ⅛" (.3 cm) strips for shutters. Place a shutter on each side of the windows. Texture the shutters with lines from your precision screwdriver.

16 THE ROOF

Mix a 1⅛" (2.9 cm) ball of Bronze, a ⅞" (2.2 cm) ball of White and a ¾" (1.9 cm) ball of Gray clay (or the equivalent blocks) for the roof tiles.

17 Mix the roof clay only until marbleized. Do not mix completely. Roll the mixture through your pasta machine to the no. 5 setting. Next run it through the small noodle attachment of the pasta machine.

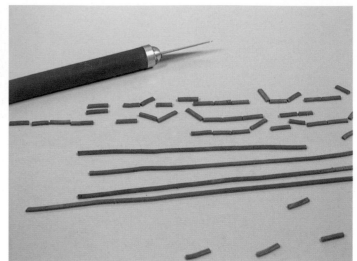

18 Place the roof noodles on a ceramic tile and cut various-sized pieces from ⅛" (.3 cm) to ⅜" (1 cm) in length.

19 When I place the roof shingles, I put my fingers on the opposite side of the roof. To avoid ruining the detailed shingles, I suggest you do only the back roof at this time so you can bake it before doing the front roof.

On the back roof of the manor, place pieces of roof shingles in various lengths along the bottom edge. Press the top edges firmly to the roof with your finger, the Clay Shaper or the handle of your needle tool. Continue to add rows the same as before until you reach the top of the roof. Do the same with one side of the door-addition roof.

Add a sidewalk at the front door made from the wall mixture clay. Texture the same as you did the walls.

Bake one hour.

20 THE WINDOWS AND DOOR

Use Midnight Blue clay for your front door. Add a Victorian Copper petite glass bead for the door handle. Use the roof base mixture for your window frames. Follow the optional window frame instructions on page 22.

21 THE GRASS

Add the grass to Wellington Manor.

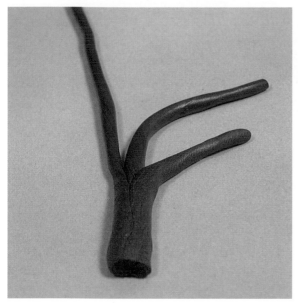

22 THE TREE TRUNK

Mix a ½" (1.3 cm) ball of Bronze, a ⅜" (1 cm) ball of Gray and a ⅜" (1 cm) ball of Black clay for a tree trunk. Roll the mixture into a snake. Cut it into three pieces. Place the three pieces together on one end and press together to create the tree trunk.

23 Place your tree trunk at the back right corner of the manor. Make a 2" (5.1 cm) and a 1" (2.5 cm) pancake of clay. Twist the 2" (5.1 cm) pancake and place it on the roof on top of the tree limbs. Add the 1" (2.5 cm) pancake on top of the other.

24 FINISH THE ROOF

Complete the front roof the same as the back, and finish the second side of the door roof. Recondition the roof clay and run it through your pasta machine to the no. 6 setting. Using the Victorian-edged roller, cut out a piece of roof clay approximately ½" (1.3 cm) wide and at least the length of the manor. Place on the roof peak going over the edge. Trim. Do the same for the door roof peak.

Bake one hour.

25 THE TREE LEAVES

Using Leaf Green and the lighter value Leaf Green mixture, put teardrop-shaped leaves on the bottom edges of the clay base of your tree. It is helpful to hold the project in your hand so it can be turned upside down. That way you can easily see where to place the leaves.

26 Continue to cover your tree with leaves until the base does not show.

Check your tree and add more leaves on top of the other leaves until you are happy with the look. I did not like the look of the top of the trunk of my tree, so I added leaves to the tree trunk to cover the part I didn't like.

To protect the tree, you can bake the manor for one hour at this time. It depends on how you work when doing the bushes. For example, I tend to crush the tree leaves because I put my fingers where they do not belong.

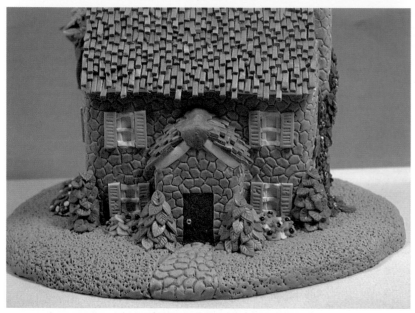

27 THE BUSHES

Put a cone of clay on the front corners of the manor. Cover the clay with medium green mix heart-shaped leaves.

Place a small pancake of clay under the front windows. Cover with heart-shaped leaves made with the light green mixture. Using Orange clay, make flowers for these bushes. Use a Black petite glass bead in the centers of the flowers.

Make a cone of clay for the corners of the door addition. Cover with Leaf Green teardrop-shaped leaves. Use the lighter Leaf Green mixture on these bushes, also.

28 Now use dark green teardrop-shaped leaves to create a vine going up the chimney. Place Lavender flowers on this vine and use Old Rose petite glass beads in the centers of these flowers.

29 Place two small cones of clay between the windows at the back of the manor. Cover the cones with teardrop-shaped leaves using your grass mixture.

Make a snake of clay and place it around the bushes. Cover with dark green heart-shaped leaves. Add Bordeaux Red flowers. Place a small ball of Yellow clay in the centers of the flowers.

30 Place two small pancakes of clay on the base between the windows on the left side of Wellington Manor. Cover them with teardrop-shaped leaves made from dark green and the lighter value of this mixture. Make small balls of Yellow clay and place them on these bushes. Do a final baking of two hours.

Glue Hunter Green felt to the bottom of Wellington Manor. If desired, add the window glow. Wellington Manor is now finished.

Rockport Lodge

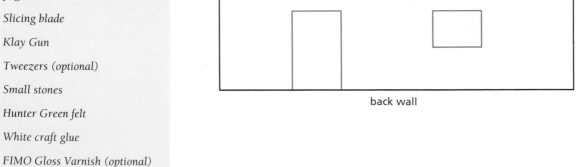

Rockport Lodge is a log building with a large stone fireplace. The stone walkways leading to the front and back doors give the lodge a homey feeling and seem to invite guests in for a cozy evening before the fire.

The front addition adds to your basic building techniques.

MATERIALS

Polymer clay
- Anthracite
- Black
- Bronze
- Carmel
- Champagne
- Fir Green
- Golden Yellow
- Green
- Lavender
- Leaf Green
- Navy Blue
- Ochre
- Red
- Terra Cotta
- White
- Yellow

Mix Quick

Petite glass beads
- Black 42014
- Gold 40557
- Rainbow 40374
- Royal Plum 42012

The must-have tools listed on page 9

Slicing blade

Klay Gun

Tweezers (optional)

Small stones

Hunter Green felt

White craft glue

FIMO Gloss Varnish (optional)

DOOR & WINDOW PATTERNS

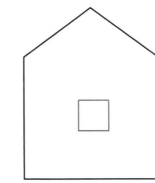

right side

front end

front door

front wall

left side wall

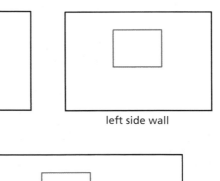

back wall

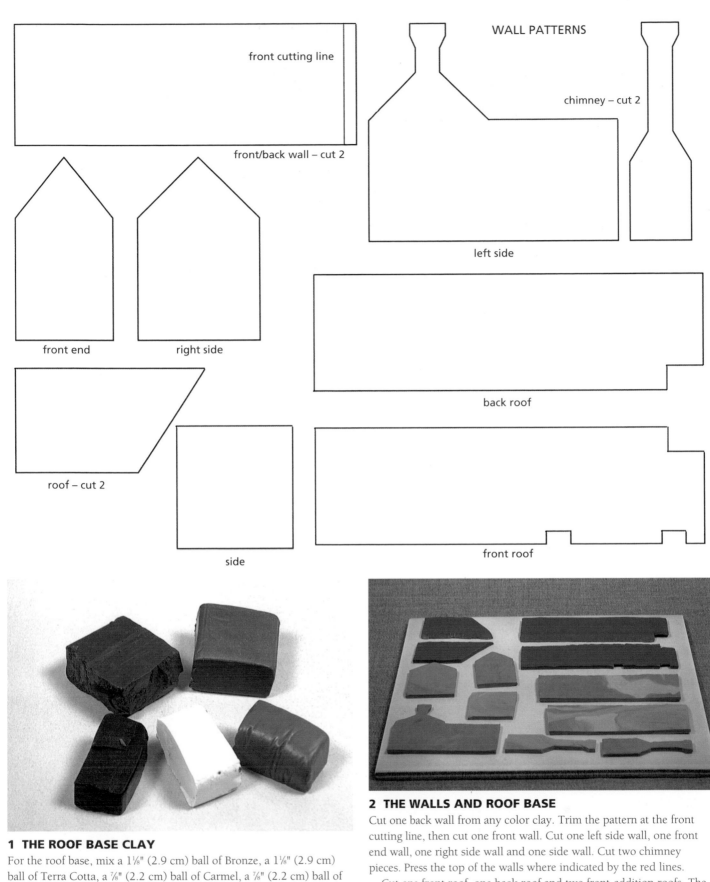

front cutting line

front/back wall – cut 2

WALL PATTERNS

chimney – cut 2

left side

front end

right side

back roof

roof – cut 2

side

front roof

1 THE ROOF BASE CLAY

For the roof base, mix a 1⅛" (2.9 cm) ball of Bronze, a 1⅛" (2.9 cm) ball of Terra Cotta, a ⅞" (2.2 cm) ball of Carmel, a ⅞" (2.2 cm) ball of White and a ⅞" (2.2 cm) ball of Black clay (the equivalent blocks shown here). After cutting the roof base, save a ¾" (1.9 cm) ball of clay for the doors and windows. The rest of this clay will be used for the log walls.

2 THE WALLS AND ROOF BASE

Cut one back wall from any color clay. Trim the pattern at the front cutting line, then cut one front wall. Cut one left side wall, one front end wall, one right side wall and one side wall. Cut two chimney pieces. Press the top of the walls where indicated by the red lines.

Cut one front roof, one back roof and two front-addition roofs. The lodge roofs will look like they are backward because you are looking at the underside of the roofs. Turn over one roof addition piece and press to 45 degrees where indicated.

Bake all foundation pieces for one hour.

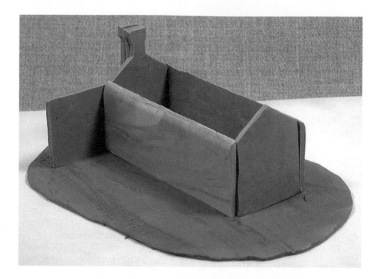

3 THE BASE AND FOUNDATION

Form a flat 4¾" x 6" (12.1 cm x 15.2 cm) base for Rockport Lodge from any color clay. I ran my base clay through the pasta machine on the no. 1 setting to get it really flat; however, if you do this, you will not be able to press the walls into the base very much. If you are comfortable with doing the under color, you can create the base this way. Otherwise, get the base as flat as you can by pressing a second ceramic tile on top of the clay.

Follow the instructions from Wellington Lodge, page 63, to put the chimney pieces on the left side wall.

Place the back wall into the base. Now place the left and right side walls in the base. Anchor the walls with clay. Next put the front wall into the base and anchor it, also.

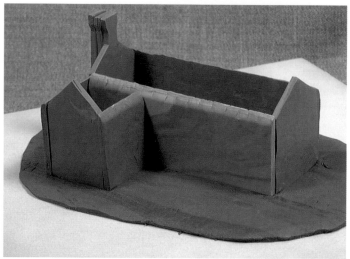

4 Put the front end wall and side wall into the base and anchor them.

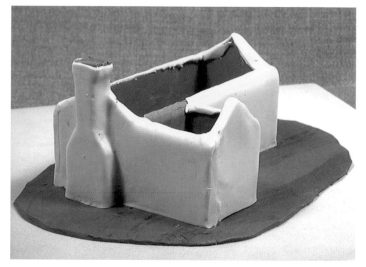

5 THE UNDER COLOR

Put the under color around the walls, trimming it at the top. If you have a Clay Shaper, use it to press the under color around the chimney.

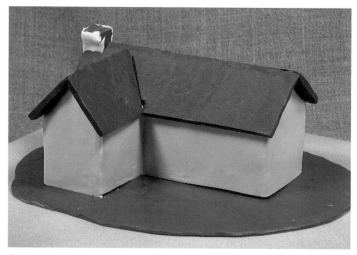

6 Place the front and back roof pieces on the lodge. If necessary, trim the roof pieces with your craft knife to get a good fit. Now put the front-addition roof pieces on.

Bake for one hour.

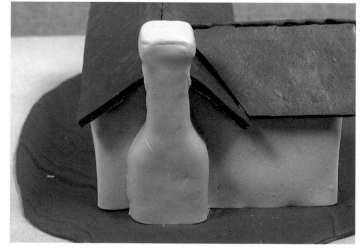

7 THE CHIMNEY

Run Champagne clay through your pasta machine to the no. 4 setting. Place it around your chimney, including the top. This color will also be used for the sidewalks.

8 Find some small, multicolored stones. (I collected mine by sweeping a driveway.) Wash and dry them, and then firmly press the stones into the clay on the chimney. The clay will be forced up around and between the stones, helping to anchor them.

Be sure to put some stones on the sides of your chimney. Sometimes a pair of bent tweezers are helpful. You may now want to bake your lodge for one hour. When I tried to do the next step without baking first, I knocked the stones out as I worked on the logs.

If a stone falls out after you've baked the lodge, use a good white craft glue such as Aleene's Thick Designer Tacky Glue to glue the stone back into place.

9 THE LOG WALLS

Mix the remainder of the roof base clay with a ⅞" (2.2 cm) ball of Golden Yellow and a ⅞" (2.2 cm) ball of Mix Quick. Use your Klay Gun with the disc that has seven holes. Press out the logs for your lodge. If you don't have a Klay Gun, roll out logs to ⅛" (.3 cm) thickness.

Following the numbers on the diagram below left, put a log along each of the odd-numbered walls. Cut the logs so that they stop at the wall edges.

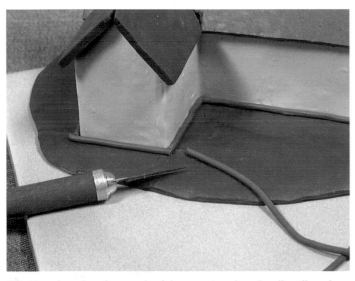

10 Next, lay a log along each of the even-numbered walls. Allow the logs to extend past the wall edges to the edge of the logs already laid.

11 Now place a log on the even-numbered walls, not extending past the length of the wall. Gently press these logs onto the previous ones.

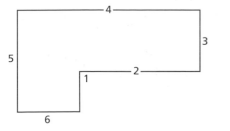

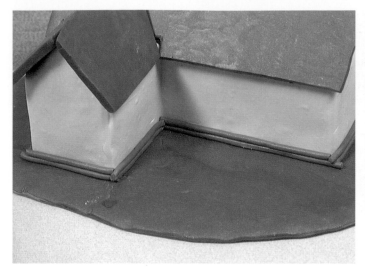

12 Next, place a log on the odd-numbered walls, extending past the wall to the edge of the even-numbered wall logs. I find it easiest to cut the logs to the correct length before I place them on the walls. However, if you prefer, you can place the logs first, and then put your chisel blade under the log and use your craft knife to cut the logs to the desired length.

Continue in this pattern until the walls are complete. As you work, pick up the lodge and make sure the logs are fitting snugly. Press the logs down if any under color is showing.

13 If the last logs under the eaves do not place easily, you can hold the lodge in one hand and place the log under the eaves on one end. Let it slide into place. If necessary, pull it into place with your needle tool. Place logs next to the chimney and snug against the roof peak.

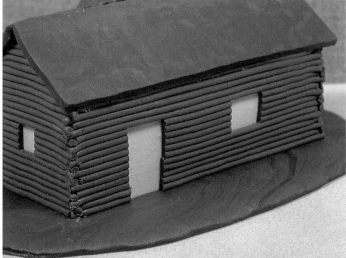

15 Cut the other doors and windows the same as before.

14 THE WINDOW AND DOOR OPENINGS

Using the door and window patterns, cut the front door, front wall window and right side window. It is easiest to use your chisel tool to cut the openings. On this project, you only need to cut the sides of the door and windows with your chisel; then just remove the pattern and pull out the cut logs. If there is a log at the top or bottom of the opening that is only partially cut, finish cutting through the log and remove it.

16 THE SIDEWALK

Using the Champagne clay, lay a sidewalk from the front door to the edge of your base. Press real stones into the sidewalk.

17 Also lay a sidewalk at the back door. I made mine go past the base slightly. Press stones into this sidewalk and bake the lodge for one hour.

18 Roll the clay saved from the roof base through your pasta machine to the no. 4 setting. Press this clay into your doors. Use a Gold petite glass bead for the door handles. For the windows, cut ¹⁄₁₆" (.2 cm) strips from this clay and put them in the windows for the frames, using the slicing blade method on page 22.

Next, put your grass on the base of Rockport Lodge.

19 THE ROOF

Mix a 1⅛" (2.9 cm) ball of Bronze and a ⅞" (2.2 cm) ball of Black clay just until marbleized. (Do not mix completely.) The equivalent blocks are shown here.

20 Run this clay through your pasta machine to the no. 6 setting and then through the large noodle attachment. Press the strips with your Scotch-Brite pad and finish texturing them with your sharp needle tool. Cut lengths between ⅛" (.3 cm) to ⅜" (1 cm) for the shingles. Place on the roof, starting at the bottom. Stagger the shingles when placing them to create more interest.

21 Where the peaks come together, the shingles will need to be trimmed to fit. Complete the main roof before the addition. Place the shingles on the addition tight to the main roof so that spaces where your roofs do not fit exactly will not show.

22 Place shingles at the peaks, staggering them slightly. If there are any bare spots where the shingles did not fit completely or didn't cover something you wanted them to, cover them with a few shingles.

When the roof is complete, go over the shingles slightly with your sharp needle tool. This blends the peak shingles and gives the others a rougher look.

23 Be sure to fit the shingles on the main roof snug against your chimney. Bake for one hour.

24 THE VINES
Use the dark green and lighter value of this mixture to make teardrop-shaped leaves for the vine at the front of the lodge. Carry this vine over the windows at the front, around the corner by the door, and then up onto the roof.

25 Use Apricot clay for the flowers on this vine. Place Rainbow petite glass beads in the center of each flower.

26 Place a small amount of clay under the eaves by your chimney. Use a mixture of the leaf colors in the teardrop shape to create a vine on your chimney. Carry this vine over the roof and around the chimney.

27 Use Lavender clay with Royal Plum petite glass bead centers for flowers on this vine.

28 Place one small cone of clay at the corner by the front door and another cone on the right side. Cover them with Leaf Green teardrop-shaped leaves.

Put a small pancake of clay under the front window and cover it with light green mix heart-shaped leaves.

Next, put a small pancake of clay at the right front corner and cover it with dark green teardrop-shaped leaves.

29 Place Red clay flowers on the bush under the front window.

Use Pink clay flowers at the front corner. Put a Royal Plum petite glass bead in the center of each flower.

30 Using light green heart-shaped leaves, create a bush under the window at the back of the lodge. Carry this bush up the wall slightly and over the grass.

31 Use Red clay with Black petite glass bead centers for flowers on this bush.

32 Place a ball of clay under the window next to the chimney and cover it with heart-shaped medium green leaves.

33 Use Yellow clay for the flowers on this bush. Put a Black petite glass bead in the center of each flower.

34 Now do a final baking for two hours. When cool, cover the bottom of Rockport Lodge with Hunter Green felt.

If you like the look, give a glow to the windows. Rockport Lodge is now finished.

La Casita

La Casita means "the little house." I included this project for a change of style in your village. The stucco walls and tile roof give it the look of a Spanish hacienda.

The tile roof is made differently than the rest of the village. This will build on your basic experience.

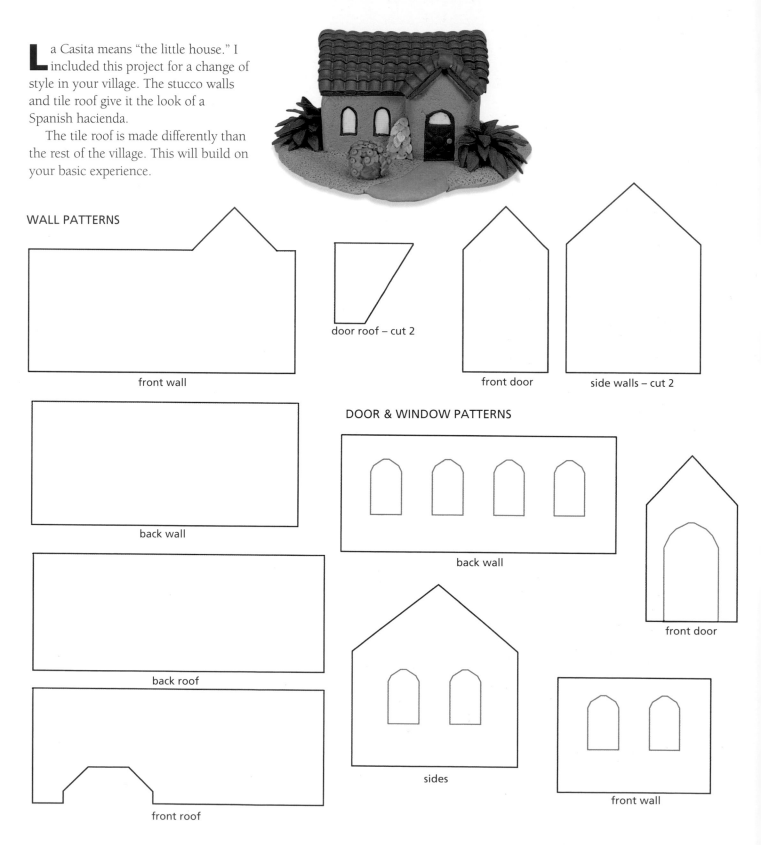

WALL PATTERNS

door roof – cut 2

front wall

front door

side walls – cut 2

back wall

DOOR & WINDOW PATTERNS

back wall

front door

back roof

front roof

sides

front wall

MATERIALS

Polymer clay
- Anthracite
- Black
- Bordeaux Red
- Bronze
- Carmel
- Fir Green
- Gold
- Golden Yellow
- Green
- Leaf Green
- Navy Blue
- Ochre
- Orange
- Terra Cotta
- White
- Yellow

Mix Quick

Petite glass beads
- Cream 40123

The must-have tools listed on page 9

Klay Gun

26-gauge wire

Wire cutters

Tin foil

Native American Friendly Design Impression—sunburst

Hunter Green felt

White craft glue

FIMO Gloss Varnish (optional)

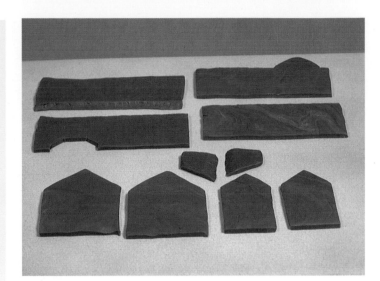

1 THE WALLS AND ROOF BASE

From any color clay, cut one front wall, one back wall, two side walls and two front extensions. Using Carmel clay, cut one front roof, one back roof and two front-extension roof pieces.

Turn over one front-extension roof so the peaks are together. Press the top of the front/back walls and the roof peaks.

Bake all foundation pieces for one hour.

2 THE BASE AND FOUNDATION

Create a thin pancake of any color clay approximately 4" x 5" (10.2 cm x 12.7 cm). You may want to create an uneven front like I did.

Run some clay of any color through your pasta machine to the no. 5 setting and place it on a piece of parchment paper. Lay the front door extension pieces on the clay and cut around them. Place them on the front wall.

Insert the walls into your base and cover with the under color. Place the roof on your house and bake for one hour.

3 THE WALLS

Mix a 1⅛" (2.9 cm) ball of Carmel, a ⅞" (2.2 cm) ball of White and a ⅞" (2.2 cm) ball of Yellow clay with a ⅞" (2.2 cm) ball of Mix Quick. Make a pancake and roll through your pasta machine to the no. 5 setting. Cover your walls with this clay and texture them with your Scotch-Brite pad. Cut the window and door openings.

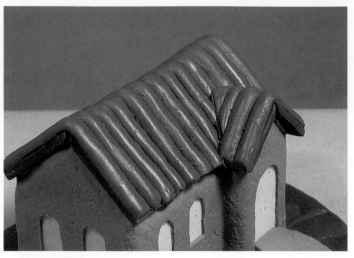

4 With the wall mixture, make a sidewalk leading from the front door; texture it the same as you did the walls.

5 THE ROOF

Mix a 1⅛" (2.9 cm) ball of Carmel with a ⅝" (1.6 cm) ball of Mix Quick. Put some of the mixture through your Klay Gun, using the half-moon disc. Place these semicircular strips on your roof from the front roof edge, over the peak, to the back roof edge. Repeat this procedure for the door addition.

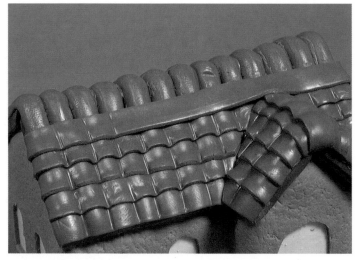

6 Condition the remainder of the roof mixture and run it through your pasta machine to the no. 5 setting and then through the large noodle attachment. Starting at the bottom left edge of the roof, lay one noodle along the roof edge. Press between the half moons with your Clay Shaper.

Lay a second noodle, slightly overlapping the first, and press this one, also. Continue in this manner until the front and back roofs are complete.

7 Lay a last noodle along the peaks of the roof and press down. Bake for one hour.

8 THE WINDOWS AND DOOR

Run some Terra Cotta clay through your pasta machine to the no. 5 setting. Add the front door. Cut out a window in the top of the door. I created a pattern in the door with a Friendly Design sunburst impression. If you do not have one, look around your house to find something that can create an impression, such as a rubber stamp or a piece of jewelry. Use your imagination!

9 For the window frames, cut strips from the Terra Cotta clay or use the slicing blade method on page 22.

10 THE GRASS

Next, place the grass around your house.

11 THE FLOWERPOT

Mix a small amount of wall clay with a small amount of Terra Cotta and make a ½" (1.3 cm) ball. Place it at the corner of your sidewalk and press in the center to form a flowerpot.

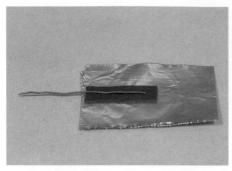

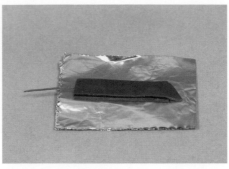

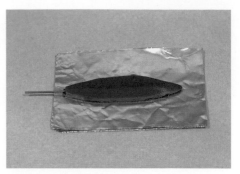

12 THE LEAVES

Cut strips of tin foil about ½" x 1" (1.3 cm x 2.5 cm). Cut pieces of wire about ¾" (1.9 cm) to 1" (2.5 cm) long. Run some dark green clay mixture through your pasta machine to the no. 5 setting. Cut a strip of clay and place it on the tin foil. Place a piece of wire on the clay, extending it over the edge.

13 Place another piece of clay on top of the first and press them together.

14 Cut the joined strips into a long leaf shape. Make veins in the leaf with your sharp needle tool.

15 Hold the leaf between your fingers and shape it. Continue making leaves, varying their length from ½" (1.3 cm) to ¾" (1.9 cm) long. It will take approximately forty to fifty leaves to make the two bushes on this project.

Bake the house and the leaves for one hour.

16 THE BUSHES

Place a ball of clay between the windows at the center of the left side. Press the leaves into the ball, making sure the clay on the leaf goes into the clay of the ball—this will help hold the leaves on. If desired, you can put white craft glue, such as Aleene's Thick Designer Tacky Glue, on the wire before placing the leaves. Continue placing leaves, starting at the bottom and going around the ball of clay.

17 Alternate the placement of leaves as you make additional rows until the bush is complete.

Add another bush at the front right corner of the house similar to the one on the left side.

18 Place medium green heart-shaped leaves into your flowerpot in the front. You may want to place a small ball of clay in the pot first to help fill it.

19 Make very small balls of Orange clay and put them on the bush in the flowerpot.

Place a cone of clay in the corner by the door and cover it with light green teardrop-shaped leaves.

20 With Leaf Green teardrop-shaped leaves, create a meandering bush at the back right corner.

21 Use Bordeaux Red flowers on this bush. Place a Cream petite glass bead in the center of each flower.

22 Bake for two hours. Cover the base of La Casita with Hunter Green felt. If desired, put a glow in the windows. La Casita is now finished.

Shaw Manor

Shaw Manor is a wonderful Tudor-style home, featuring wooden beams with plaster inserts and stone over the wooden front door and on the chimney. It is much easier to build than it appears.

Think how wonderful Shaw Manor will look in your village.

WALL PATTERNS

chimney – cut 2

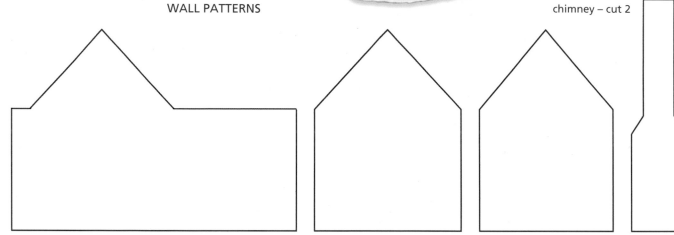

front wall

front extension – cut 2

side walls – cut 2

back wall

back roof

DOOR PATTERN

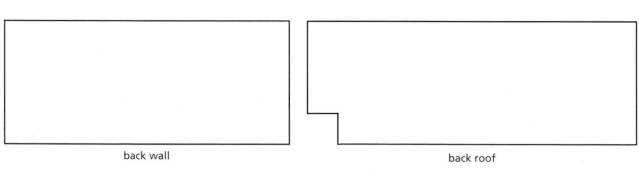

extension roof – cut 2

front door

front roof

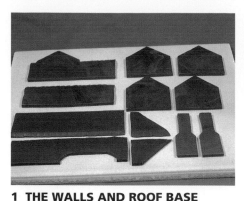

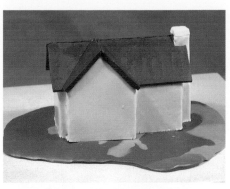

1 THE WALLS AND ROOF BASE

From any color clay, cut one front wall, one back wall, two side walls, two front-extension walls and two chimney pieces.

Using Terra Cotta clay for the roof base, cut one roof front, one roof back and two front-extension roof pieces.

Bake for one hour.

2 THE BASE AND FOUNDATION

Make a 4½" x 5½" (11.4 cm x 14 cm) base for Shaw Manor.

Run any color of clay through your pasta machine to the no. 5 setting. Place the chimney pieces and front-extension pieces on the clay and cut around them. (See the instructions for Pine Crest Cabin on page 54.) Put the chimney pieces on one side wall and the front-extension pieces on the front wall. Press the walls into the base and cover with the under color.

Place the roof pieces on. Bake for one hour.

3 THE WALLS

Use Terra Cotta clay for the beams on your manor. Condition this clay and run it through your pasta machine to the no. 5 setting. Cut ¼" (.6 cm) strips, using a slicing blade if you have one. If not, use your craft knife.

Place a beam along both edges of the roof peak, cutting them at the roof edges. Put beams vertically down the sides of the front extension. Place another beam horizontally across the front, creating a triangle with the beams you placed at the peak. Add another horizontal beam along the base and one more about a ½" (1.3 cm) up. Next, place two vertical beams between the horizontal beams, as shown. Add diagonal crosspieces in the peak. Place a beam on the front wall, to the left of the extension.

4 Add beams on the left side the same as you did for the front. The only difference is that the two vertical beams are closer together.

MATERIALS

Polymer clay
- Anthracite
- Apricot
- Black
- Bronze
- Carmine
- Champagne
- Fir Green
- Golden Yellow
- Green
- Jasper
- Lavender
- Leaf Green
- Navy Blue
- Ochre
- Terra Cotta
- White
- Yellow

Petite glass beads
- Black 42014
- Bottle Green 45270
- Victorian Gold 42011
- White 40479

The must-have tools listed on page 9

WireForm Impression Mesh Copper no. 8116

Hunter Green felt

White craft glue

5 Place a beam across the top and bottom of the back wall. Cut an opening for the door in the bottom beam. Next, place vertical beams down the sides of the back wall and on both sides of the door opening. Use two more vertical beams to frame the window opening to the left of the door. Put a beam along the top of the door and window. Finally, add diagonal crossbeams in the other spaces.

Texture all the beams with your sharp needle tool to give them a wooden look.

6 THE STONES

For the stones, mix a ⅝" (1.6 cm) ball (or equal block) of Bronze, a ⅝" (1.6 cm) ball of Champagne and a ⅝" (1.6 cm) ball of Jasper clay just until marbleized. Roll the clay through your pasta machine to the no. 4 setting.

7 Lay the mixture on a ceramic tile and cut strips of varying widths.

8 On one of the strips, cut "soldier" stones for the top of the door by alternating every other stone between a **V**-shape and an inverted **V**. (Shown in the middle row in this picture.) Cut the other stones in varying widths.

Bake the entire manor and your stones for one hour.

9 THE PLASTER WALLS

Run a ⅞" (2.2 cm) ball of Champagne clay mixed with a 1⅛" (2.9 cm) ball of White clay through your pasta machine to the no. 4 setting. Use the same technique used to create doors (steps 31–33 on page 21) to press the clay into the openings made by the beams on the front wall. Remove the clay and cut out the impression. Place the cut pieces into the opening. Use your Clay Shaper or a pencil eraser to texture the "plaster." Leave the center open for your window.

10 Do the same for the side wall, except leave the side squares open for your windows.

11 Add the plaster to the back wall, leaving the under color showing in the door and window openings.

12 Recondition the Champagne clay mixture and run it through your pasta machine to the no. 4 setting. Cover the right-side front wall. Cut the arched door opening.

Cover the right side and chimney with the Champagne clay mixture.

13 THE WINDOWS

Using scissors, cut a piece of the copper mesh to fit the window opening on the front wall. Place ¹⁄₁₆" (.2 cm) strips of Terra Cotta clay over the mesh around the outside edges of your window. Also place a piece down the center of the window. Texture the window frame with your needle tool. Do the same for the window at the back of Shaw Manor.

15 THE STONE WALLS

Place the "soldier" stones over the front door, pressing them firmly into the wall clay. Now add stones of different sizes to the rest of the front wall, side wall and chimney.

17 THE DOORS

Run Terra Cotta clay through your pasta machine to the no. 4 setting. Make a front door. Run a small amount of the clay through your pasta machine, again to the no. 5 setting. Cut two strips ¹⁄₁₆" (.2 cm) wide to use as crosspieces in the door. Use a Victorian Gold petite glass bead as a doorknob.

14 Now do the windows on the left side, omitting the center piece.

16 THE SIDEWALK

Put a sidewalk at the front and back doors, using the Champagne clay mixture. Bake the manor for one hour.

18 Use the same method to make a back door. The Terra Cotta clay darkens when baked, so your door will match the beams after baking.

19 THE ROOF

To make roof shingles, condition Bronze clay and run it first through your pasta machine to the no. 5 setting and then through the large noodle attachment. Texture the strips with your Scotch-Brite pad and a sharp needle tool. Cut into pieces about ⅛" (.3 cm) to ⅜" (1 cm) wide. Place the shingles in an uneven pattern on the roof, starting at the roof edge. Go over the shingles again with your sharp needle tool.

20 Finish the front and back roof. Cut two pieces about ½" (1.3 cm) long and trim one end into a **V**. Place one piece on the peak edge of the front extension. Cover the rest of the peak with shingles. Do the same for the main roof peak.

21 THE GRASS

Place grass around the manor and texture. Bake for one hour.

22 THE BUSHES

Place a narrow cone of clay at the left door edge. Cover it with teardrop-shaped leaves made with the lighter value of the Leaf Green mixture.

Put a piece of clay along the front wall and cover it with heart-shaped medium green leaves. Put a snake of clay for a hedge along the edge of the base at the front. Add another small one on the other side of the sidewalk.

23 Use dark green teardrop-shaped leaves for a vine that wanders around the chimney and wall.

24 Put a small snake of clay at the back wall and cover it with heart-shaped leaves made with the grass mixture and a lighter value of the grass mixture.

25 Create a bush on each left-side corner similar to the bush at the front door.

Add a slightly larger bush between the windows using light green heart-shaped leaves.

Put two small pancakes of clay between the bushes. Cover them with teardrop-shaped leaves made from the grass mixture.

26 Cover the snake (step 22) with dark green teardrop-shaped leaves. Use Apricot for flowers on the bush at the front of Shaw Manor. Place a Bottle Green petite glass bead in the center of each flower.

27 Place Yellow clay flowers with Black petite glass bead centers on the vine on the chimney.

28 Make the flowers for the bush at the back from Carmine clay. Use White petite glass beads for the centers.

29 Place Lavender flowers on the low bushes on the left side of Shaw Manor.

Bake the manor for two hours. When cool, glue Hunter Green felt on the bottom. Shaw Manor is now completed.

chapter six

Village Finishers

Village Church

The Village Church is the very center of the village. Imagine the voices, raised in prayer, coming from within and the light shining through the stained glass windows.

Your basic building techniques will be increased by the steeple and stained glass windows.

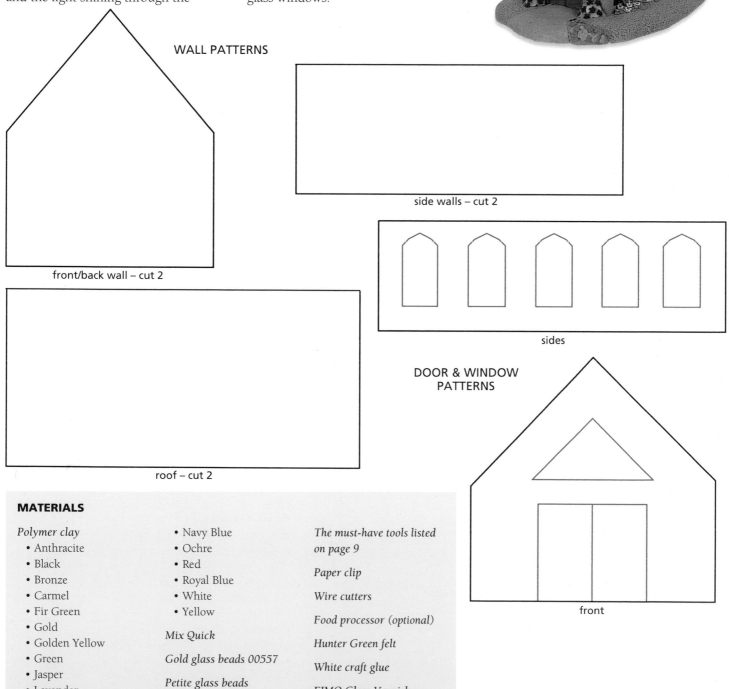

WALL PATTERNS

front/back wall – cut 2

side walls – cut 2

sides

roof – cut 2

DOOR & WINDOW PATTERNS

front

MATERIALS

Polymer clay
- Anthracite
- Black
- Bronze
- Carmel
- Fir Green
- Gold
- Golden Yellow
- Green
- Jasper
- Lavender
- Leaf Green

- Navy Blue
- Ochre
- Red
- Royal Blue
- White
- Yellow

Mix Quick

Gold glass beads 00557

Petite glass beads
- Ginger 42028

The must-have tools listed on page 9

Paper clip

Wire cutters

Food processor (optional)

Hunter Green felt

White craft glue

FIMO Gloss Varnish

1 THE WALLS AND ROOF BASE

From any color clay, cut two side walls and two front/back walls.

Mix three-fourths of a block of Bronze clay with one-fourth of a block each of White and Ochre clay. Cut two roof pieces from this clay.

Press the top of the side walls and the roof peak to 45 degrees. Save the rest of the roof clay mixture for use on your church.

2 THE CROSS

Roll Gold clay through your pasta machine on the no. 1 setting. Cut a cross 1⅛" tall X ¾" wide (2.9 cm X 1.9 cm).

Cut a ½" (1.3 cm) length of a paper clip with wire cutters. Press one end of the cut piece into the bottom of your cross. Bake the cross and foundation pieces for one hour.

3 THE FOUNDATION

Make a 4¼" X 6¼" (10.8 cm X 15.9 cm) pancake base from any color clay. Set the walls into the base and anchor them.

Cover the walls with the under color clay and put the roof on.

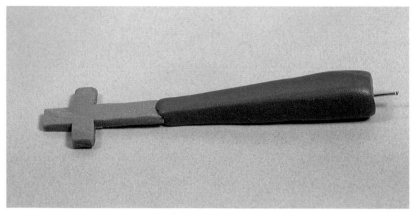

4 THE STEEPLE

Create a 2" (5.1 cm) long steeple from the roof clay mixture. Taper it so the base is ½" (1.3 cm) wide and the top is ¼" (.6 cm) wide. Press the cross into the top of the steeple.

Cut another piece of the paper clip ½" (1.3 cm) long. Press it into the center at the bottom of the steeple.

Bake the church and steeple for one hour.

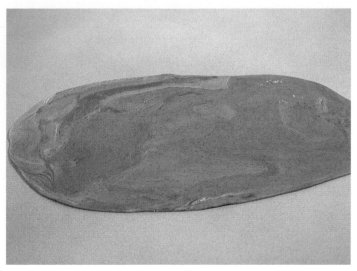

5 THE WALLS

For the walls, mix a ⅞" (2.2 cm) ball each of White, Carmel, Golden Yellow and Jasper clay with a 1" (2.5 cm) ball of Mix Quick (or the equivalent blocks). Mix the colors only until marbleized.

6 Run the clay mixture through your pasta machine to the no. 5 setting. Put the clay on your church walls.

7 THE WINDOW AND DOOR OPENINGS AND SIDEWALKS

Cut out the window and door openings. Make a sidewalk with the wall clay. Texture the walls and sidewalk with your Scotch-Brite pad.

Take a ball of wall clay and place it on the roof peak. Form this into a square with a flat top. Place the steeple into the clay and bake for one hour.

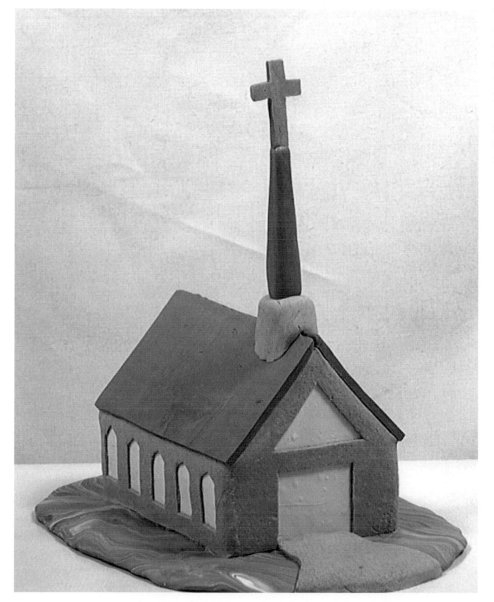

8 THE STAINED GLASS WINDOWS

Take a ¾" (1.9 cm) ball each of Yellow, Red, Royal Blue and Green clay and put the balls into a food processor. Process them until the clay is chopped into small pieces. If you do not have a food processor you can dedicate solely to your claywork, you can crumble the clay and then chop it with your craft knife.

Place the mixture on a ceramic tile. To warm this mixture, place your hand on the clay and hold it until the clay is warm. It helps if you pat the clay and warm the ceramic tile by placing it on your lap or on a Clay Warmer, if you have one.

9 Once the window clay is warm and it releases from the tile, hold it between your palms until the clay sticks together. Run this clay through your pasta machine to the no. 5 setting.

10 Fill the church windows with your stained glass mixture. Use the roof mixture for the doors of your church. With your needle tool, draw a line down the center of the door to create two doors. Add Gold glass beads for the door handles.

11 Condition some Black clay and run it through your pasta machine to the no. 6 setting. Cut very thin strips, about ½₂" (.1 cm) wide, of Black clay. Place a strip of Black around the outside of the windows. Put a strip down the center of each window. Anchor a strip ¼" (.6 cm) from the top on the center strip and pull the end up to the top of the window side. Repeat on the other side of the center strip. Also place a strip horizontally across the windows, approximately ¼" (.6 cm) from the bottom of each window.

12 On the front window, place a strip of Black around the outside of the window. Starting at the center of the window, place three pieces of Black from the center out to the window edges (these pieces will form a **Y**-shape). Finally, place a short piece diagonally across the corners of the window.

13 THE GRASS

Add the grass around your church.

14 THE ROOF

Recondition the roof clay and run it through your pasta machine to the no. 6 setting. Next, run it through the large noodle attachment. Texture it with your Scotch-Brite pad and your sharp needle tool. Cut various pieces ⅛" (.3 cm) through ¼" (.6 cm) wide.

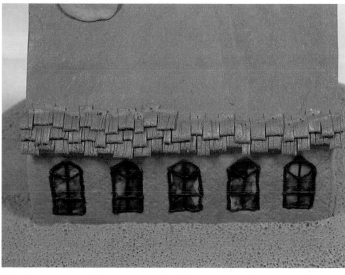

15 Place the roof tiles on your church roof.

16 When both sides of the roof are completed, cut one strip to a peak and place it over the edges of your roof. Continue placing roof tiles on the peak until it is completely covered.

17 THE STEEPLE

Pull on the steeple slightly. If it comes off, put some Aleene's Thick Designer Tacky Glue or another good white craft glue on the paper clip and a little on the steeple. Replace the steeple and allow the glue to dry. Cover the steeple with roof tiles, starting at the bottom and going to the top.

18 THE TREE TRUNK

Form some Bronze clay into a snake. Cut it into three pieces. Line the three pieces up side-by-side and press them together at the bottom only. Place this tree on the back wall of the church, slightly off center. Splay the loose ends of the three pieces and press them to the church. Add a couple of smaller branches. Texture with your needle tool to create the tree bark.

Bake for one hour.

19 THE TREE

Roll some Green clay into a snake and flatten it. Place this clay at the top of your tree trunk.

21 Be sure to carry the leaves over the roof.

20 Cover your tree top with teardrop-shaped leaves made from the dark green mixture. Completely cover the base clay. Keep putting leaves on top of the others until you are happy with your tree shape.

22 THE BUSHES

Place a small ball of clay on each side of the front door. Using the light green leaf mix, cover the bushes with teardrop-shaped leaves.

With heart-shaped Leaf Green leaves, make a small bush at the corner of the sidewalk, near the base.

23 Create bushes along the sides of your church with Leaf Green teardrop-shaped leaves. Carry some of the leaves between a few windows.

24 Place some clay around the base of the tree at the back of your church. Using leaves in the lighter value Leaf Green mixture, make a bush on that clay.

Put a cone of clay next to your tree trunk and cover it with heart-shaped light green leaves.

25 On the bushes next to the front door, use Red clay flowers.

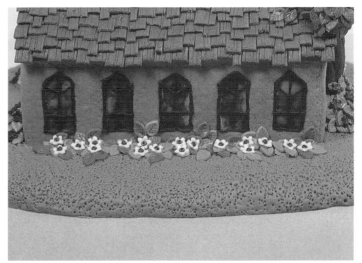

26 Use Yellow flowers on the bushes at the sides of your church. Place a Ginger petite glass bead in the center of each flower.

27 Place Lavender flowers on the bush around the tree trunk at the back of your church.

Bake for two hours. Place Hunter Green felt on the bottom of the church.

For this project, I recommend you put FIMO Gloss Varnish on the stained glass windows to make them shine. The Village Church is finished.

Matthew's Grocery

Every village needs a grocery store like Matthew's Grocery. This is a wonderful, old-time neighborhood grocery. People can find anything they need here, and the owner loves to chat with all his customers while he fills their orders.

Remember to stop outside and get some of the wonderful produce displayed there.

MATERIALS

Polymer clay
- Anthracite
- Apricot
- Black
- Bordeaux Red
- Bronze
- Fir Green
- Golden Yellow
- Granite
- Gray
- Green
- Leaf Green
- Navy Blue
- Ochre
- Red
- Terra Cotta
- Violet
- White
- Yellow

Mix Quick

Petite glass beads
- Black 42014

The must-have tools listed on page 9

Decoupage glue

Fine-point permanent black marker

Eye shadow

Sand

Paint brush

Blush brush

Hunter Green felt

White craft glue

FIMO Gloss Varnish (optional)

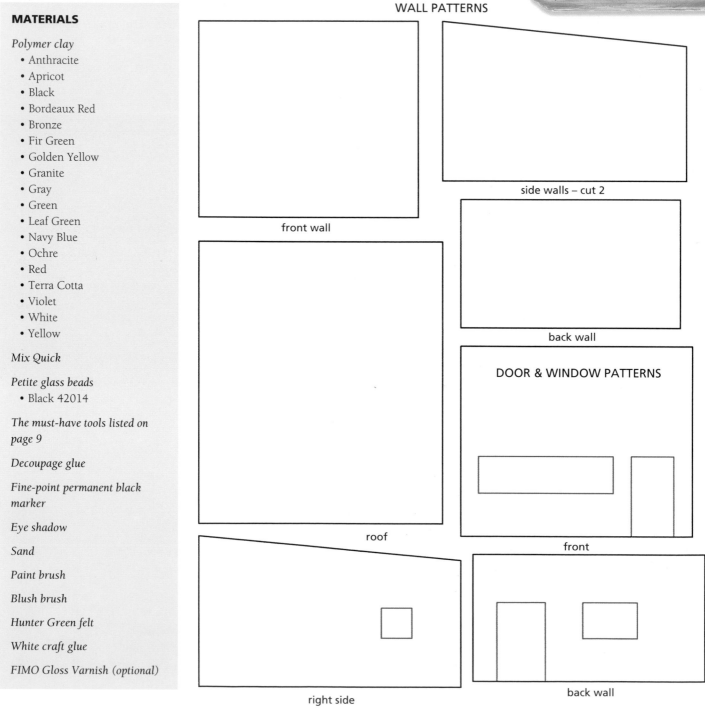

WALL PATTERNS

side walls – cut 2

front wall

back wall

DOOR & WINDOW PATTERNS

roof

front

right side

back wall

1 THE FOUNDATION

From any color clay, cut one front wall, one back wall and two side walls. Cut one roof base from Black clay. Bake for one hour.

Make a pancake of any color clay, approximately 3½" X 4" (8.9 cm X 10.2 cm). Place the walls in the pancake and cover with the under color. The under color should go over the top of the front wall and down the back side about ½" (1.3 cm). Place the roof on as shown.

2 Trim the front and sides of the base so that they are straight. Bake for one hour.

3 THE WALLS

Mix a ⅞" (2.2 cm) ball each of White, Black and Granite clay with a ¾" (1.9 cm) ball of Mix Quick just until marbleized. The equivalent blocks are shown here. Cover the walls with this mixture.

4 THE WINDOW AND DOOR OPENINGS

Cut the front door and window openings.

5 Cut the small window on the right side and the door and window opening on the back wall.

With your needle tool, create a stone look in the walls.

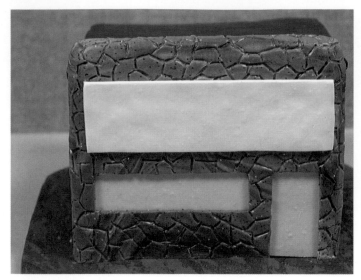

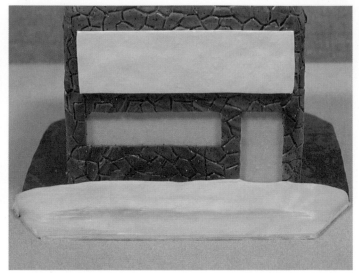

6 THE SIGN

Roll White clay through your pasta machine to the no. 5 setting. Cut a ⅝" x 2¼" (1.6 cm x 5.7 cm) rectangle. Place this on the front wall, above the door and window, as shown.

7 THE SIDEWALKS

Mix a ⅝" (1.6 cm) ball of White with a ⅝" (1.6 cm) ball of Gray clay for your sidewalk. Cut one edge straight and place it at the front of your grocery. Press the sidewalk down over the edge of the base and out about ½" (1.3 cm).

8 Put a sidewalk at the back door also, and bake for one hour.

9 THE WINDOWS AND DOORS

Run Red clay through your pasta machine to the no. 5 setting. Place the clay into the door opening. Cut out a window in the door with your chisel tool. Cut strips of Red clay ⅛" (.3 cm) wide using a slicing blade. Place the strips around your sign and the front window frame.

10 Repeat for the back door and window frames. Use a Black petite glass bead for the door handles.

11 THE ROOF

Run Black clay through the pasta machine to the no. 5 setting, and use it to cover the roof. Sprinkle sand on the roof and press it into the clay.

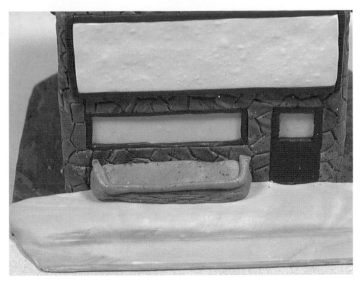

12 THE PRODUCE BINS

For your produce bins, mix a ½" (1.3 cm) ball of wall color with a ¾" (1.9 cm) ball of Ochre clay until almost completely mixed. Place a block under the front window. Roll a small snake and place it around the edge of the block.

13 Make three balls of this clay in different sizes to create barrels near your produce bin. I used my Clay Shaper to form the holes in my barrels.

14 THE GRASS

Put grass on the sides and back of Matthew's Grocery. Bake for one hour.

15 THE PRODUCE

Use a small amount of grass clay to make a watermelon about ½" (1.3 cm) long. Pick up some dark green eye shadow on a large blush brush and dab the watermelon. Next, create some broken lines with a fine-point permanent marker. Place your watermelon next to the produce bins.

Make a few apples using Bordeaux Red clay. Place Bronze stems in your apples and put them in the barrel on the right.

With Golden Yellow, make a bunch of bananas and place them in the center of your produce bin, allowing them to hang over your watermelon. Draw a few black lines on the bananas with the fine-point permanent marker.

Mix a ½" (1.3 cm) ball of Orange with a ½" (1.3 cm) ball of White clay and create a pile of oranges. Use a small amount of eye shadow on your oranges. Place them at the right side of your produce bin.

16 Make some peaches with Apricot clay and place them in the larger barrel at the left. Make the tomatoes in the other barrel with Red clay.

Now make a bunch of grapes with Violet clay, another bunch with Bordeaux Red clay and the last bunch with the grass clay mixture. Place them in the produce bin.

18 On the other side wall, press a snake of clay along the bottom of the wall. Mix a ¾" (1.9 cm) ball of grass clay with a ¾" (1.9 cm) ball of White clay and make teardrop-shaped leaves. Place them on the wall to create your bush.

17 THE BUSHES

Put a pancake of clay at the center of the left wall and cover it with light green teardrop-shaped leaves.

19 Have the leaves wander on the wall at different heights. Bake for two hours.

20 THE SIGN

Photocopy the Matthew's Grocery sign at right, or make your own by hand or on a computer. Cut to fit the clay sign area, using a craft knife and ruler. Cover the white of the sign on the front of your store with decoupage glue.

21 Place the paper sign over the clay sign. Cover the sign with the decoupage glue. Glue Hunter Green felt on the bottom of your grocery store. If you want to, put a glow in Matthew's Grocery's windows. The store is now completed.

The Lighthouse

The Lighthouse sits on the hillside above your village, a beacon protecting ships entering the harbor. It has stone steps leading to the door and a granite cliff on the back side.

The lighthouse starts differently than the other cottages in your village and will add to your basic skills.

DOOR & WINDOW PATTERNS

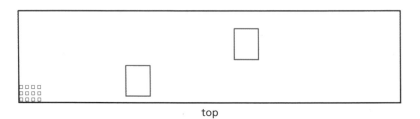

top

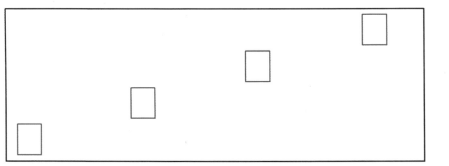

middle

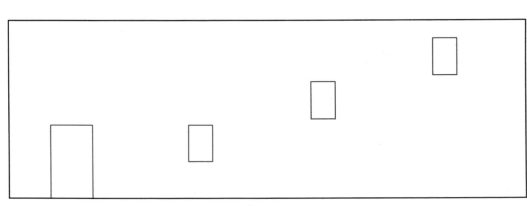

bottom

MATERIALS

Polymer clay
- Anthracite
- Black
- Bordeaux Red
- Bronze
- Fir Green
- Golden Yellow
- Granite
- Gray
- Green
- Leaf Green
- Navy Blue
- Ochre
- White
- Yellow

Petite glass beads
- Black 42014

The must-have tools listed on page 9

1" (2.5 cm) wooden dowel

Tin foil

Saw

Hunter Green felt

White craft glue

FIMO Gloss Varnish (optional)

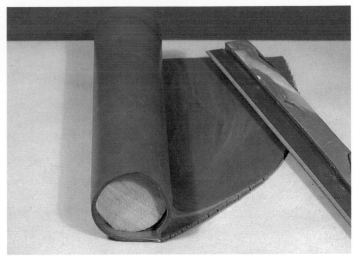

1 THE FOUNDATION

Cut a 5" (12.7 cm) length of a 1" (2.5 cm) dowel. Condition any color clay and run it through your pasta machine to the no. 4 setting. Cut a strip 5" (12.7 cm) wide. Cut one edge straight. Lay the dowel on the clay.

2 Roll the clay over the dowel. Press the cut edge slightly to the other side to create an impression where they meet. Unroll the edge and cut along the impression.

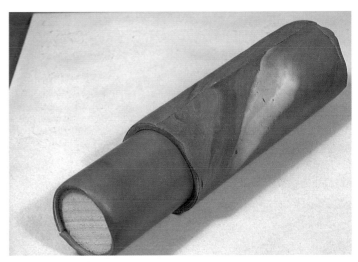

3 Press the cut edges together.

4 Cut a 3½" (8.9 cm) width of clay. Place it on the dowel on one edge the same as you did on the first piece.

5 Repeat the above procedure with a strip 1⅞" (4.8 cm) wide. Trim the clay at the bottom and top if needed.

6 THE TOP

From a ball of Black clay, form a top for your lighthouse 1¼" (3.2 cm) wide and peaking at the top.

Bake the top and lighthouse foundation for one hour.

7 THE BASE

Make a firm ball of tin foil. Press the top and bottom flat. Roll any color clay on the no. 1 setting of your pasta machine. Cut a piece larger than your foil ball. Place the foil on top of the clay and cover it with another piece of clay. Smooth the clay base.

9 Cover the lighthouse with the under color, carrying it over the top. Place the roof on your lighthouse.

Bake for one hour.

8 Place your lighthouse on the base.

10 THE WALLS

Roll Black clay through your pasta machine to the no. 5 setting. Cover the bottom section of your lighthouse and texture the clay with your Scotch-Brite pad. Use the pattern for windows around the bottom portion, placing the door pattern where you have room for the walkway. Cut out the door opening.

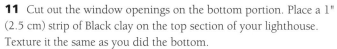

11 Cut out the window openings on the bottom portion. Place a 1" (2.5 cm) strip of Black clay on the top section of your lighthouse. Texture it the same as you did the bottom.

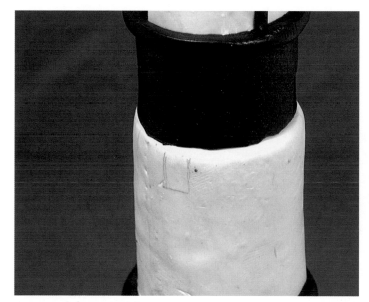

12 Using the center window pattern strip, center the left window over the door. Wrap the pattern around the center section and lightly pencil the top right window on the pattern. This will aid you in the placement for windows on the top section. Match the blue square on the top section window pattern with the penciled window, and then cut the window openings. Erase the pencil marks on the center section as much as possible.

13 Place a ¹⁄₁₆" (.2 cm) wide strip of Black clay above the top Black section. Cut ¹⁄₃₂" (.1 cm) strips of Black clay and place four vertical strips evenly spaced around the top. Cover the bottom of the roof with Black clay.

14 THE ROOF

Cover the top of the roof with Black clay and texture with your Scotch-Brite pad.

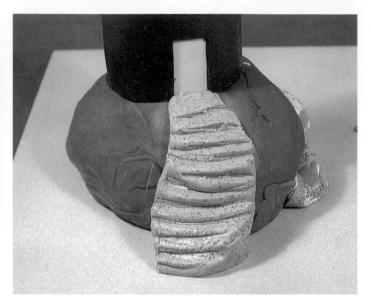

15 THE STEPS AND WALK

Mix half a block of Granite clay with a 1⅛" (2.9 cm) ball of White and a ⅞" (2.2 cm) ball of Gray. Make a walkway and steps from the door to the bottom of the base. Use your chisel tool to make the steps.

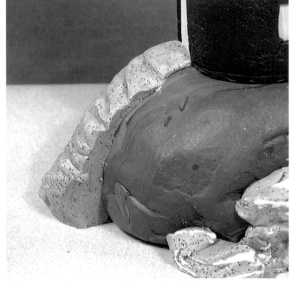

16 To get the steps small enough, I had to extend the clay out from the base. Cut your edges, if needed.

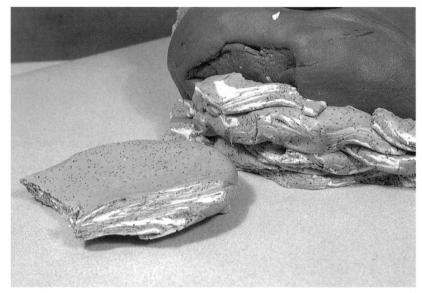

17 THE ROCKS

Take the remainder of the sidewalk clay and mix it slightly with a ⅞" (2.2 cm) ball of White clay. Press the clay into a pancake and break off pieces for the rock walls. Place rocks on one side of the base, starting at the bottom. The more uneven your rocks are, the more interesting they will be.

Save some of the rocks for later.

18 My base curved in, so I filled it out with some clay between the rocks and the steps around the base.

Bake the lighthouse and extra loose rocks for one hour.

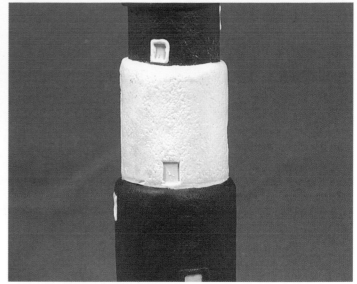

19 THE REMAINING WALL

Cover the center portion of your lighthouse with White clay that has been run through your pasta machine to the no. 5 setting. Centering the left window over the door, cut out the window openings.

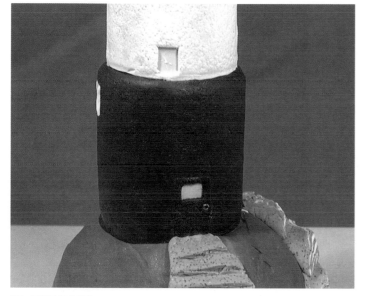

20 THE DOOR

Use Red clay for your door. Cut a window in the door and use an Antique Gold glass bead for the doorknob.

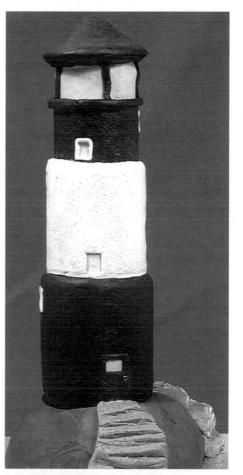

21 THE WINDOW FRAMES

Use some of the White clay for the window frames in the Black sections.

22 THE GRASS
Place the grass clay on the base of your lighthouse.

23 Press the remaining rocks into your grass around the base.

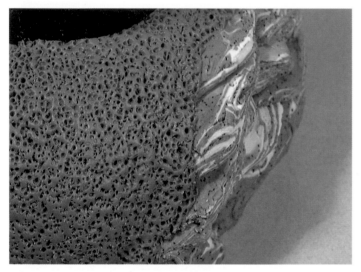

24 Carry your grass over the edges of the rocks on the base. Texture the grass on the rocks with your needle tool so it blends with the rest of the grass.

Bake for one hour.

25 THE CENTER WINDOWS
Use Black clay that has been run through your pasta machine to the no. 5 setting for the window frames in the White portion of your lighthouse.

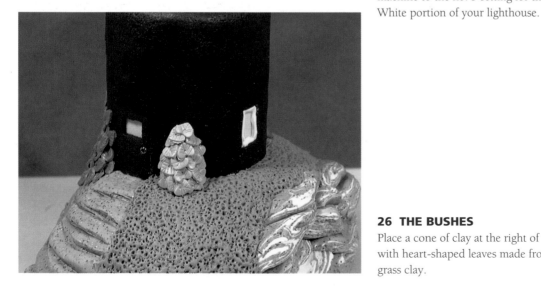

26 THE BUSHES
Place a cone of clay at the right of your door and cover it with heart-shaped leaves made from a lighter value of the grass clay.

27 Press a snake of clay about two-thirds of the way around your lighthouse, starting at the left side of your door and ending about at the center window. Make a bush going up the lighthouse and onto the base with Leaf Green teardrop-shaped leaves.

28 Mix a ½" (1.3 cm) ball of Bordeaux Red with a ⅜" (1 cm) ball of White clay just until marbleized. Use this color for the flowers on this bush. Place Black petite glass beads in the center of each flower.

29 Use dark green teardrop-shaped leaves to make a vine on your rocks and grass.
   Bake for two hours.

30 Put Hunter Green felt on the bottom of your lighthouse. I recommend putting a glow in the lighthouse windows. Your lighthouse is now completed.

Foliage & Accessories

To finish your village, it's fun to add trees, bushes, park benches, fences, brick walls and lampposts. These are just a few of the items that you can make. Use your imagination to add to your village. You can work on the accessories while your cottages are baking.

THE PINE TREE

You can create free-standing pine trees to place around your village. Follow the instructions for the pines in Pine Crest Cabin on page 59.

MATERIALS FOR THE PINE TREE

Dark green leaf clay mixture

Tools listed in basic instructions

THE BUSHES AND FLOWERS

You can also create free-standing bushes and flowers to help fill in your village. They can be made by themselves or added to a small grass base. Follow the basic instructions in chapter three.

MATERIALS FOR THE BUSHES AND FLOWERS

Any color green mixture desired

Any color for the flowers

Tools listed in basic instructions

MATERIALS FOR THE PARK BENCH

Polymer clay
- Bronze
- Gray
- Leaf Green
- Ochre
- White
- Yellow

Tools listed in basic instructions

1 THE PARK BENCH

Run a mixture of White and Gray clay through your pasta machine on the no. 1 setting. Cut two supports from this clay, ⅝" wide x ¾" tall (1.6 cm x 1.9 cm), with a seat cutout.

Run Bronze clay through your pasta machine to the no. 3 setting and make six wooden planks 1" long x ⅛" wide (2.5 cm x .3 cm).

Bake for twenty minutes.

2 Make a base of grass and place the supports in the clay about ¾" (1.9 cm) apart. Place a thin strip of clay on the supports, and then put on the wooden planks.

Bake for twenty minutes

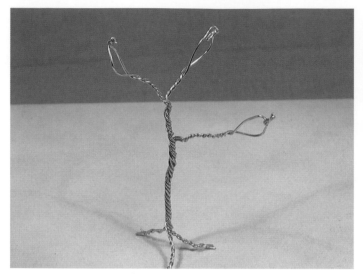

1 THE DECIDUOUS TREE

Cut six 5" (12.7 cm) pieces of 20-gauge wire. Starting ½" (1.3 cm) from one end, twist the wires together for about 2½" (6.4 cm). On the ½" (1.3 cm) roots, twist three groups of two wires together. On the other end, take two wires and twist them together for a branch. Twist the other four wires together for about ½" (1.3 cm), then split them and make two more branches. Leave about 1" (2.5 cm) untwisted. Spread them apart and twist the ends. This gives support for the top of your tree.

2 Wrap the twisted tree trunk and branches with strips of tin foil; the polymer clay won't stick to the wires. Place the tree in a clay base, pressing the roots in firmly. Wrap the tree trunk with Bronze clay strips that have been run through your pasta machine to the no. 6 setting.

Bake for thirty minutes.

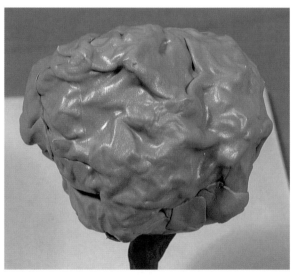

3 Make a ball of tin foil and place it on the top of your tree. If the ball is uneven, this will give your tree more interest.

4 Run Leaf Green clay through your pasta machine to the no. 6 setting. Wrap the foil with this until all the foil is covered.

MATERIALS FOR THE DECIDUOUS TREE

Polymer clay
- Bronze
- Carmel
- Grass green mixture
- Leaf Green
- Terra Cotta

Tin foil

30" (76.2 cm) of 20-gauge wire

Tools listed in basic instructions

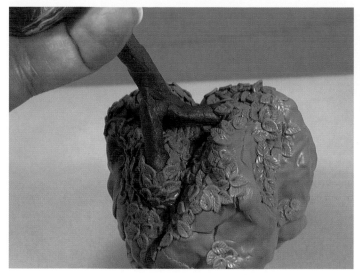

5 Starting at the bottom of your tree, place leaves on the clay foundation.

6 It seems to work best if I make uneven circles with leaves, and then fill them in. This helps me keep the leaves from all going in the same direction.

7 After the top of the tree is covered, place grass around the base. I added some wood chips to the base of my tree by chopping a little Carmel, Bronze and Terra Cotta clay together.

Bake for one hour. My tree started to fall over as it was baking, so I had to prop it up with a glass jar. You may need to prop your tree by placing something next to it for it to lean on. Check on your tree during and after the baking process until the clay is completely hardened.

MATERIALS FOR THE ARCH

Polymer clay
- Bronze
- Carmine
- Dark green leaf mixture
- Gray
- Leaf Green
- Ochre
- White
- Yellow

Tools listed in basic instructions

1 THE ARCH

Flatten Bronze clay to ¼" (.6 cm) thick. Cut a strip 3" (7.6 cm) long and form an arch. Bake for twenty minutes.

2 Make a base of grass clay. Place the arch in the center and press it to form indentations. Remove the arch and place a thin mixture of White and Gray clay on the base for a sidewalk. Fit the sidewalk between the arch markings. Replace the arch firmly.

Place a vine of dark green leaves on the arch and base. Use Carmine clay for the flowers on this vine.

Bake for thirty minutes.

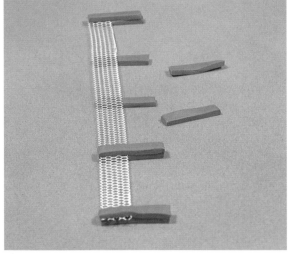

1 THE WIRE FENCE

Cut a strip of contour mesh ⅜" wide X 5½" long (1 cm X 14 cm), or whatever length desired. Mix White and Gray clay and run it through your pasta machine to the no. 5 setting. Cut ten pieces ⅛" wide X ½" long (.3 cm X 1.3 cm). Place five strips on a ceramic tile, put the wire on top and press the remaining five strips of clay on top of the previous strips and wire.

Bake for twenty minutes.

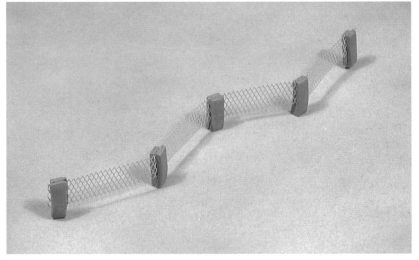

2 Bend the wire between the posts and stand your fence up.

MATERIALS FOR THE WIRE FENCE

Polymer clay
- Gray
- White

WireForm Contour Mesh Aluminum

Tools listed in basic instructions

MATERIALS FOR THE WOOD AND WIRE FENCE

Polymer clay
- Bronze
- Leaf Green
- Ochre
- White
- Yellow

28-gauge wire

Tools listed in basic instructions

1 THE WOOD AND WIRE FENCE

Roll a log of Bronze clay ¹⁄₁₆" (.2 cm) wide. Cut fence post pieces ½" (1.3 cm) long.

Bake for twenty minutes.

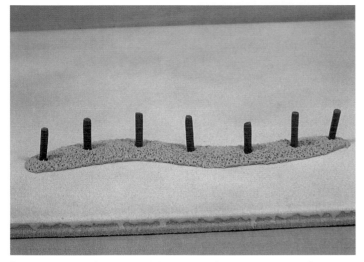

2 Make a base of ³⁄₁₆" (.5 cm) thick grass clay and place your fence posts into the grass.

Bake for twenty minutes.

3 Twist a piece of 28-gauge wire three times the length of your fence to one end post. Wrap the wire around each fence post to the other end. Wrap it around the end post several times and then take the wire back to the first post, wrapping around each post as you go. Twist the wire on the post and cut the excess. If the posts come out of the base, glue them back in and allow the glue to dry before wrapping the wire.

MATERIALS FOR THE STONE WALL

Any color clay for the stones

Tools listed in basic instructions

THE STONE WALL

Mix any color clay desired for stones. Break off small pieces and make a rough ball. Place it on a ceramic tile. Continue until your stone wall is complete.

Bake for thirty minutes.

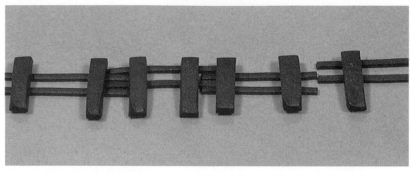

MATERIALS FOR THE WOODEN FENCE

Polymer clay
- Bronze
- Leaf Green
- Ochre
- White
- Yellow

Tools listed in basic instructions

1 THE WOODEN FENCE

Run Bronze clay through your pasta machine to the no. 3 setting. Cut as many ⅛" X ⅝" (.3 cm X 1.6 cm) fence posts as you want, cutting in multiples of two. Run the remaining clay through your pasta machine to the no. 5 setting. Cut the same number of ¹⁄₃₂" X 1" (.1 cm X 2.5 cm) boards as you cut posts.

Place two boards on a ceramic tile slightly less than ⅛" (.3 cm) apart. Put two posts on the boards about ⅛" (.3 cm) from the ends. Put a board on the tile between the others and one below. Place two posts on these boards. Repeat until you have used all your fence posts.

Bake for twenty minutes.

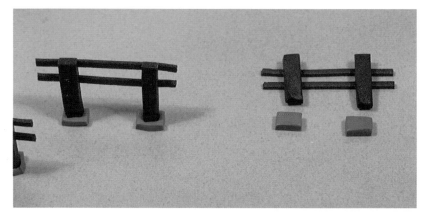

2 Cut small pieces of grass clay slightly larger than your fence posts. Place them by pairs on your ceramic tile and stand the fence piece from step 1 on the base.

Bake for twenty minutes.

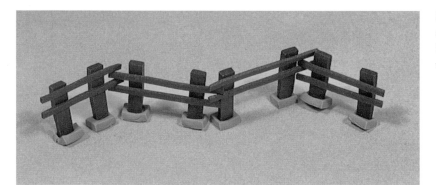

3 To display your wooden fence, alternate the direction of the fence pieces and stand them anywhere desired.

MATERIALS FOR THE LAMPPOSTS

Polymer clay
- Black
- White
- Yellow

⅛" (.3 cm) wooden dowel

½" (1.3 cm) square beads with holes

Black craft paint

FIMO Gloss Varnish (optional)

Tools listed in basic instructions

1 THE LAMPPOSTS

Cut 2¼" (5.7 cm) pieces of a ⅛" (.3 cm) wooden dowel. Make lamppost tops with your under color clay and press the post into the bottom to form a hole. Bake the top for twenty minutes.

2 Put Black clay on the bottom and top of the under color clay. Cut four strips ¹⁄₃₂" (.1 cm) wide by the length needed. Bake for twenty minutes.

Paint the wooden lampposts and base with black craft paint. Put the posts into the base. Put white glue on the top of the wooden posts and place your lamp top on the post. Allow to dry.

Coat the lamp top with FIMO Gloss Varnish, if desired.

MATERIALS FOR THE BRICK WALLS

Any color clay for the walls

Tools listed in basic instructions

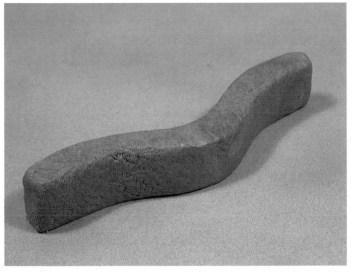

THE WALLS

You can create brick walls to match your cottages. Make a base of any color clay ¼" thick X ½" high (.6 cm X 1.3 cm) in any length desired. Bake the base for twenty minutes.

Cover the base with the wall color clay. Texture the wall to match the cottage. If desired, add a nameplate to your wall.

Bake for twenty minutes.

chapter seven

Variations

Once you've created all the projects in this book, you may wish to expand your village with different styles and colors of houses. You may even want to recreate your own home—or the homes of family and friends—in polymer clay

Here are a few examples of how you can change the look of some of the projects in this book to come up with something totally different. Try changing one to suit your own tastes.

MAKING A COTTAGE FROM SCRATCH

If you want to model your own home in polymer clay, it's best if you have a photograph to work from. Start by drawing the front door on a piece of graph paper, using one of the door patterns in this book to get the scale correct. (If you're adding this house to your village and have changed the scale of your houses, be sure to reduce or enlarge this pattern accordingly.)

Determine where the first window closest to the door would sit. Is it one door-width away? Two door-widths? Now judge the width and height of the windows against the door's width and height. Draw in the windows. Next, judge how far the roof is from the top of the door. Make this the top of your front wall. Finally, deter-mine how far the edges of the walls are from the windows or doors. Draw the side and back walls in the same manner, and then cut the pieces out.

When cutting your foundation walls, make the front and back walls slightly smaller to allow for the added width of the under color and wall color clay. Also make the end walls slightly smaller to allow for the thickness of the front and back walls. You may have to experiment with the roof size to get it to match. Don't get discouraged if it doesn't fit the first time! If the pieces are too large, cut them down with a craft knife. If they are too small, you will need to remake them. Experiment until you are pleased with the results.

SUNNY COTTAGE VARIATION

Sunny Cottage is probably the hardest project to make look different. When the walls are as short as Sunny's, there is only so much you can do!

Changing the doors and windows adds variety. You don't have to limit yourself to varying colors or styles. You can extend the front and back walls of any of the patterns; just remember to lengthen the roof the same amount. Changing the width or height of the side walls is a little more challenging. It changes the pitch of the roof, so you will have to do a little experimenting.

The original Sunny's Cottage.

In this variation I changed the wall clay to a light brown mixture made with White, Carmel and Terra Cotta clay. I textured the walls with the Scotch-Brite pad. The door is now Midnight Blue. I also changed the shingle color to a mix of Terra Cotta and Bronze clay, omitted the chimney, varied the size and placement of the windows, added shutters made from the door color and changed the foliage and flowers.

Here I changed the wall and sidewalk color to a light gray mixture made by mixing White and Granite clay just until marbleized. I substituted rounded stones made with my chisel tool for the square stones. I changed the roof to Black shingles and extended the chimney. The door is now Red clay. I also reversed the door and window pattern on the front and added additional windows to the side. On the front window, I omitted the center window frame bar. To further the variation, I used different colors and groupings of foliage and flowers.

LAMBERT'S HOME VARIATION

This home was changed by moving the door addition to the left side and centering it. The two sidewalks no longer connect. This really changed the look without changing the pattern.

The original Lambert's Home.

Here I used a mix of Gray and Bronze clay for the walls, textured with a Scotch-Brite pad. I used Rosewood clay for the roof foundation and window trim. The door is a mixture of Champagne and White clay. The roof shingles are made from Bronze clay.

LA CASITA VARIATION

This variation requires a little more modification of the pattern. I moved the door to the center. To do this, the front wall and front roof patterns needed to be modified.

The original La Casita.

Here I moved the front door and used Gray clay for the walls. I textured the walls with a piece of netting. The roof foundation and roof are made with Bronze clay. I also added Black shutters and a Bordeaux Red door.

ADDITIONAL MEASUREMENTS

PANCAKE THICKNESSES

Here is a list of the clay thicknesses created by the various settings on my pasta machine. Since not all pasta machines are the same, compare the thickness of the clay sheets produced by each of your pasta machine settings to mine and adjust, if necessary. If you do not have a pasta machine, use these measurements to roll the appropriate thickness of clay. The pasta machine setting is given on the left, and the equivalent pancake thickness appears on the right.

no. 1 setting	3⁄32" (.24 cm)
no. 2 setting	no measurable difference from no. 1
no. 3 setting	5⁄64" (.2 cm)
no. 4 setting	1⁄16" (.16 cm)
no. 5 setting	3⁄64" (.12 cm)
no. 6 setting	1⁄32" (.08 cm)

ADDITIONAL BALL SIZES

If you have a circle template from AMACO, the ball sizes not given can be cut as follows:

To get the equivalent of a 3⁄4" (1.9 cm) ball, combine a 5⁄8" (1.6 cm) ball and a 1⁄2" (1.3 cm) ball.

To get the equivalent of a 1" (2.5 cm) ball, combine a 7⁄8" (2.2 cm) ball and a 5⁄8" (1.6 cm) ball.

I want to thank the following companies for graciously allowing me to use their products. The brands used in this book are as follows:

AMACO
FIMO Polymer Clay
FIMO Gloss Varnish
Polymer Clay Template
NuBlade kato
Marxit kato
Clay Shaper

Gay Bowles Sales, Inc.
Mill Hill Glass Beads
Mill Hill Petite Glass Beads

Kemper Tools
Klay Gun
Clay Cutters
Stylus
Wire brushes

Excel Hobby Blade Corp
Craft knife
Chisel blades
Precision screwdrivers
Stylus

Kunin Felt
Classic Rainbow Felt

Aleene's
Thick Designer Tacky Glue

Paragona Art Products
WireForm Impression Mesh Copper
WireForm Contour Mesh Aluminum

Fiskars
Fiskars 45mm Rotary Cutter
Fiskars Victorian Rotary Cutter blade

If some of the FIMO colors I used in my projects are not available in your area, check my Website or send a self-addressed, stamped envelope to Cottage Fever (see page 125) for a chart which gives instructions on how to mix some of the FIMO colors from other colors.

SUPPLIERS & RESOURCES

MANUFACTURERS OF POLYMER CLAY

Eberhard Faber GmbH
P.O. Box 1220
D-92302 Neumarkt/Germany
Phone: 09181/43 0-0
Fax: 09181/4 30-222
Manufacturers of FIMO and FIMO Soft.

Polyform Art Products CO.
1901 Estes Avenue
Elk Grove Village, IL 60007-5415
Phone: (847) 427-0020
Fax: (847) 427-0426
Manufacturers of Granitex, ProMat, Sculpey, Sculpey III and Super Sculpey.

T+F GmbH
RosenaustraBe 9
P.O. Box 30 12 36
D-63274
Dreieich/Germany
Phone: (0 61 03) 6 27 06
Fax: (0 61 03) 6 54 62
Manufacturers of Cernit.

MANUFACTURERS & SUPPLIERS OF CLAY-RELATED PRODUCTS

AMACO (American Art Clay Co., Inc.)
4717 W. 16th Street
Indianapolis, IN 46222
Phone: (800) 374-1600
Fax: (317) 248-9300
Website: www.amaco.com
Wholesale suppliers of FIMO, FIMO Soft, FIMO Gloss Varnish and Clay Shaper. Professional crafters contact AMACO for distributor information.

Kemper Tools
13595 12th Street
P.O. Box 696
Chino, CA 91710
Phone: (909) 627-6191
Fax: (909) 627-4008
Specializing in Cernit, Klay Gun, Clay Cutters, stylus and other clay tools.

WHOLESALE/RETAIL SOURCES

Accent Import-Export, Inc.
P.O. Box 4361
Walnut Creek, CA 94596
Phone: (800) 989-2889
Local Phone: (925) 431-1150
Fax: (925) 431-1152
Website: www.fimozone.com
Specializing in FIMO, FIMO Soft, Magic Leaf and KaleidoKane Classic Millefiori Canes. Wholesale only.

Dee's Delights, Inc.
3151 State Line Road
Cincinnati, OH 45052
Phone: (513) 353-3390
Fax: (513) 353-3933
Specializing in dollhouse and miniature supplies, FIMO, FIMO Soft, Sculpey, Super Sculpey, tools and educational supplies. Wholesale only.

Gail Ritchey
Cottage Fever
5500 Ford Crest Drive
Birmingham, AL 35242-2600
Phone: (205) 991-6869
Fax: (205) 991-3293
Website: www.cottagefever.com
Specializing in most items used in this book, FIMO, glass beads, tools. Wholesale and retail.

Wee Folk Creations
18476 Natchez Avenue
Prior Lake, MN 55372
Phone: (612) 447-3828
Fax: (612) 447-8816
Website: www.weefolk.com
Specializing in Cernit, Granitex, FIMO, FIMO Soft, ProMat, Sculpey, Super Sculpey, tools and educational supplies. Wholesale and retail.

Prairie Craft Company
P.O. Box 209
Florissant, CO 80616
Phone: (800) 779-0615
Fax: (719) 748-5112
Website: www.prairiecraft.com
Specializing in FIMO, FIMO Soft, Sculpey. Premo, Marxit, NuBlade, T-Blade, NuFlex, tools, books and videos. Wholesale and retail.

The Clay Factory
P.O. Box 460587
Escondido, CA 92046-0598
Phone: (760) 741-3242
Fax: (760) 741-5436
Website: www.clayfactoryinc.com
Specializing in Cernit, Granitex, ProMat, Sculpey, Super Sculpey, Sculpey III, tools and educational materials. Wholesale and retail.

Mill Hill
Division of Gay Bowles Sales, Inc.
P.O. Box 1060
Janesville, WI 53547
Phone: (800) 356-9438
Fax: (608) 754-0665
Specializing in glass beads and petite glass beads. Wholesale only.

Excel Hobby Blade Corp.
481 Getty Avenue
Patterson, NJ 07503
Phone: (973) 278-4000
Fax: (973) 278-4343
Specializing in craft blades and tools. Wholesale only.

Aleene's
Division Of Artis, Inc.
85 Industrial Way
Buellton, CA 93427-9528
Phone: (800) 436-7878
Fax: (805) 688-8638
Website: www.aleenes.com
Specializing in craft glues and other craft products. Wholesale and retail.

Kunin Felt
380 LaFayette Road
P.O. Box 5000
Hampton, NJ 03842-5000
Phone: (603) 929-6100
Fax: (603) 929-6180
Website: www.kuninfelt.com
Makers of Classic Rainbow Felt, Rainbow Plush Felt, Shaggy Plush Felt and Kreative Kanvas.Wholesale only.

Paragona Art Products
P.O. Box 3324
Santa Monica , CA 90408
Phone: (800) 991-5899
Local Phone: (310) 264-1980
Fax: (310) 828-8297
Makers of WireForm Expandable Mesh and WireForm Woven Mesh. Check with your local art and craft stores for Paragona Art Products. Wholesale only.

Fiskars, Inc.
7811 W. Stewart Avenue
P.O. Box 8027
Wausau, WI 54402-8027
Phone: (715) 842-2091
Fax: (715) 848-3562
Website: www.fiskars.com
Specializing in scissors, Rotary Cutters and blades, Paper Edgers, Corner Edgers and Crimpers. Wholesale only.

Dakota Clay Crafters
Cecilia Determan
26313 426 Avenue
Emery, SD 57332
E-mail: celaclay@iw.net
Creator of the Clay Extruder to use with a Klay Gun. Retail only.

I hope you enjoy this book half as much as I've enjoyed creating it. I'd love to hear from you!

Now that I am finished, I am going to make a nice "Thank-You" dinner for my family, water my plants and clean my house.

Until next time....

Gail

MATTHEW'S GROCERY

index